Battle-Ready Moms Raising Battle-Ready Kids

A Biblical Strategy for Confident Parenting

by Reba Bowman

PRESS

Battle-Ready Moms Raising Battle-Ready Kids
A Biblical Strategy for Confident Parenting
by Reba Bowman

Printed in the United States of America

ISBN 9781615796717

www.xulonpress.com

If ever there were a woman in whom there is no guile, it is Reba Bowman. She writes with the transparency, sincerity, and passion of a person who wants to share truths she deeply believes and earnestly holds dear. If you read this book, you will read the heart of Reba and be richer for it. It is my pleasure to recommend *Battle-Ready Moms Raising Battle-Ready Kids*. Your kids may hide it from you, but keep looking for it — you need to read it!

> Jan Silvious, conference speaker and author, *Big Girls Don't Whine* and *Foolproofing Your Life*

A young woman with the wisdom of the aged, Reba's insights into the emotional and spiritual needs of youth is a rare gift. She has a big heart, a passion for God's calling, and a life and message anchored in His Word. As she explores a mother's God-ordained commitment to the eternal rather than the temporal, her message to me is profound: "The condition of every child will improve or deteriorate in proportion to the ability and worth of his mother."

> Jackie Dark, speaker, and wife of former Major League baseball player and manager Alvin Dark

Reba writes with both calmness and urgency about the battle that is going on for our children. As a Marine, I wore combat boots while fighting Communism and the enemy in the jungles of Vietnam. The battle for our children, however, is a more important conflict. God does not intend for us to lose the fight. Practical and motivational, this book is one you'll want to refer to again and again.

> Tim Lee, evangelist and decorated Marine Corps veteran

To Dad and Mom

When I think of parents strapping their boots on and getting in the battle for their children, I think of you. You were out of the box before the term was popular, because you forced us to think, to know why we believed as we did, and to stand firm on those beliefs. Your relationship with God, with each other, and with me has been foundational to my life. Because of you, I am more like Him. I love you both.

Contents

❦

Acknowledgments

❧

There are so many people whom God has used to help this project to come to life. As I sit back and think of them, I realize even more fully how good God has been to me. I am so blessed to have those who push me, inspire me, and challenge me. This book would have never made it to the page without all of you.

My family: Thanks for your never-ending love and encouragement. Thanks for being in this battle with me on a daily basis. Your laughter is healing and your support means more to me than you will ever know.

Jan Silvious: Your wisdom and counsel have proved invaluable to me. Thanks for continually challenging me to think outside the box.

My editor, Lori Vanden Bosch: I can't begin to thank you enough for your wonderful touch on this book. You organized all my scattered thoughts, cut to the heart of the message, and then meshed it all back together in a way that is clear and easy to read. Your mother's touch was just what this project needed.

Ann Spangler: You were an answer to prayer. Thanks for being willing to be used in my life and in this project. Your expertise was exactly what this rookie needed to get on the right track. And thanks for the great book title.

Kay Arthur: When I was just about ready to throw in the towel on this book idea, God gave me a divine appointment with you. Thank you for taking the time to listen and give me the right advice on ministry and this manuscript. Your wisdom has kept me from making many reckless choices. Thanks for investing in me.

Thanks to Camille Platt, Brandi Johnson, Lisa Potter, and Marcia Parris. Your eye for detail and your pursuit of excellence have made a big difference in this project.

Introduction

꘏

Up until ten years ago, most of my adult life was dedicated to helping teenagers and young adults. As a coach, I have ridden thousands of miles with them, pushed them, fussed at them, encouraged them, and laughed with them. As a professor, I have challenged them, listened to them, instructed them, and rejoiced with them. As a dean, I have prayed with them, cried with them, discipled them, and eaten lots of pizza with them. It seemed as if time stood still for many years because I spent more time with young people than I did adults. I was getting older but I never felt it because it seemed like I had never left college. I was operating on their time zone and loving life.

One day God interrupted my life with a great surprise. I had just taken a new position as the dean of women at Tennessee Temple University. After years of coaching, I felt God leading me in new directions. I was settling down into a wonderful schedule of teaching, counseling, and mentoring when God brought a very special person my way. Her name was Brandi.

Brandi was a teenager from a very troubled background. As a child she had been hurt in almost every way imaginable. The state had finally interceded on her behalf and she was pulled out of her home, but unfortunately her troubles did not end there. When I met her, she was at the end of her rope and wondering if life was really worth living.

I felt a strong push from the Lord to get involved. As I began to invest in her life, I knew the Lord was asking me for more. I have to be honest; I resisted at first. I knew how to be her counselor; I knew how to be her mentor; but I felt very unqualified to fill the role of mom. I was single and had never borne any children, so how could I fill this position for someone who so desperately deserved a great home? I spent many nights face to the floor asking God to show me what to do. He did!

Brandi has been a wonderful part of my life now for over twelve years. I am so proud of her. She has fought more battles than people twice her age. With God's help she has wrestled with emotional and mental demons and won. In Christ she has been victorious. Sure, there were days of heartache, fear, and great pain. Many times I hung my head in prayer with tears dripping from my face and wondered if someone else would have done a better job. The Lord continued to reassure me that no one could do a better job because He had not given this special assignment to anyone else but me.

For every difficult day there have been ten amazing days. I still stand in awe of the healing power of God in a life. Brandi is a living testament of how God can take a life that is broken and in shambles and produce a supernatural healing. I have witnessed the miraculous in her life in so many ways. She has grown into a strong, beautiful young woman of faith. She walks with God and leans on Him one day at a time.

Today she is married to a solid, good-hearted man who loves Jesus and his family. She has four delightful boys who keep her on the move. She is involved in her local church and the ministry God has given me at Dare for More. She has reconnected with some of her siblings and has seen two of her sisters come to Christ.

I am thrilled and privileged to be a part of her life. Sometimes when people hear our story they say, "Wow, Reba, how lucky Brandi is to have you in her life." I just laugh and say, "Are you kidding me? I am the lucky one." She has brought me so much joy. She has taught me so much. And as if that wasn't enough, I have four rough-and-tumble boys who call me "Nana." Who could ask for more?

I may never be a "mom" in the traditional sense of the word, but God has given me the heart of a mother. My life with Brandi has taught me much about unconditional love, discipline, and parenting in general. Only God could know that what He would teach me through her would help so many others who were struggling. I thought of her many times as I was writing this book. Because of her I am able to say, "I have been there and if I can do it, I know you can."

Of course Brandi has not been my only source of learning. My connection with so many other wonderful kids along the way has taught me as well. As a coach I learned about instilling confidence, pushing kids to do more than they thought they could, and teaching them to deal with disappointment. As a counselor and dean I have listened to many students share their hearts and unload their stories for the first time. I have walked with young girls through crisis situations, tragedy, and pain. But I have also had the joy of being with them at their finest hours. More importantly, I have watched them grow in Christ and become strong young women of faith and virtue.

I have many memories that I cherish and still keep in touch with many of these remarkable women today. They have grown up and most of them have families of their own now. I am proud to have been a part of their lives. I love them and will never forget the special time I was able to spend with them. It is their faces that encourage me to continue going today.

God never lets me get too comfortable. After thirteen years of spending every day with young people, He rerouted my life. In a way that still boggles my mind, He pushed me out into a larger teaching ministry. Today I have the wonderful privilege to teach the Word of God to women of all ages. People ask me all the time which group I prefer working with the most, the young people or the adults. My answer is always the same: I love them both. I love the energy of the young people with their fresh ideas and spontaneity. I love the young women, the singles, and the mothers. I love the grandmothers with their wisdom, perspective, and laughter. It is my passion for both of these groups that has produced this book.

Almost a decade has passed since the day I stepped onto this new teaching platform for the first time. So many new faces flood my mind as I sit here writing today: faces of tweens who write me letters and ask for my advice on everything from boyfriends to clothes; faces of teens who email me and talk to me at conferences about dating, sex, drugs, and problems with their parents; faces of college students and young adults who want me to pray for them as they confront some of life's toughest decisions; and now I add the faces of so many mothers and grandmothers. I see their faces in my mind and hear their words as they share their concerns for their children and for themselves. They want to be good mothers. They want their children to turn out right.

I am convinced that it is possible to raise children who love God and love others with all their heart, but it won't happen accidentally. You must decide that you can make a difference. You must believe that in Christ all things are possible because it will require your all.

Recently the children's book *The Tale of Despereaux* was adapted for the big screen. It is a wonderful story about a little mouse who is very brave during a time when all other mice are cowards. He doesn't cower, he doesn't scurry. He draws pictures of cats and names them Fluffy. Despereaux is not reckless, but he is curious, and he is convinced that he can make a difference. So convinced that he takes great risks and refuses to hide from the world.

I think we can learn a lot from this mouse. In order to make a difference in the lives of children, mothers are going to have to take on these same traits. You must be brave and strong in a world where many parents are weak and afraid. You must believe in your heart that you can make a difference and then refuse to cower or scurry. Enemies are everywhere and dangers abound, but God has promised that He is greater than anything we will ever face in this world.

This book is written for mothers who have decided they are not going to sit back and hope it all works out. It's for mothers who have the courage to strap on their boots and enter the battle. It's for mothers who take their God-given responsibility as a parent seriously and refuse to relinquish their duty as watchmen on the wall.

I hope you will find in these pages the reasons to fight, the tools to fight with, and the motivation to keep fighting. I also hope you will realize that not every day is a battle. There will be moments along the way that you will stand back and rejoice in victories won. You will marvel as God uses your children in some amazing ways.

Some days God will go before you and fight the battle; you will only need to trust. Other days you will fight uphill until the sun goes down, and, as Joshua of old, you will pray for a moment more of daylight to finish the battle. In the end, it will be worth every sacrifice.

I constantly meet mothers who have one question on their minds: "What can I do?" I have prayed much about that question, and what you are about to read are the answers God gave me. I pray they will help you along the way.

Part One

My Mama Wears Combat Boots

Chapter 1

The First Sergeant

Do You Know How Important You Are?

I well remember the school playground as an elementary student. Kids running around in a frenzy jumping from one activity to the next, and teachers standing in huddled groups praying the clock would slow down for the next half hour. You always had your friends that you hung out with like a school of fish moving together in unison. These were the people that for whatever reason had accepted you and you had accepted them.

Recess time rarely came to a close before someone got into a fight or a war of words. It usually started with what we called a "slam." One kid would find a string of words that when put together and leveled at their opponent would sting like alcohol on a cut.

In my day on the elementary playground the most stinging word choices usually started with this phrase, "Your mama …" It was one thing to slam your looks or your friends, but it was another altogether to slam your mom. There was a string of "your mama" slams, and usually once they started, the fight had begun.

As I look back there was one particular "your mama" slam that seemed to get the biggest reaction, and for the life of me I don't know why. As tension would build and the slams would become more cutting, someone would step over the line and with a piercing voice yell these fatal words: *"Your mama wears combat boots!"*

With those words, fights broke out, and teachers came out of their huddle and waded into the fray of children to break up the tussle.

Where this expression came from is debated. Some say it was formed during the 1940s as women worked in factories to make war supplies. Others say it referred to women in the early wars who donned the men's military uniforms and even their boots to serve as nurses and aids on the field of battle. In the early to mid 1900s this would have been a shocking sight. But my playground years were the 1970s! Yet "your mama wears combat boots" was still the all-time favorite insult of third graders.

Times have changed and today women serve alongside men in war. "Your mama wears combat boots" is no longer a slam. In fact, today it is a positive description of a woman who is willing to fight for her country and even die for what she believes.

For that reason, I want to resurrect this phrase and instill this image in your hearts and minds. I would like "your mama wears combat boots" to be an accolade to women who are in the trenches of motherhood and are fighting to make a difference in the life of a child.

The First Sergeant

Today's mother is in a war for the lives of her children. The enemy is real and deceptive. He does not play fair and he does not care who he hurts. His weapons are varied and he has a great strategy. If our children are going to grow up and become the men and women that we want them to be, we must take this battle seriously and prepare to fight.

I am convinced that mothers are the first sergeants of their homes. First sergeants have a very important role in the daily life of each person under them. The first sergeant is the lifeblood of the military. He enforces discipline and encourages those under him. He is responsible for making sure that each person understands his role, fulfills his job, and works together with others around him. The first sergeant is also responsible for the morale and health of each soldier under his command. He must be able to communicate effectively in order to inspire, motivate, encourage, and train each man and woman. There is no area that he is not personally involved in when it comes to those who serve under him.

More than any other officer, the first sergeant has the opportunity to personally impact lives. He is often involved in helping the commander maintain discipline and standards of conduct. He is there every day and at each new obstacle. The first sergeant is a counselor, an inspector, and a supporter. He is available seven days a week, 365 days a year. He is a sounding board and confidant, and he provides the leadership that is necessary for the success of each soldier.

In his letter to the Secretary of War in 1825, Jacob Brown wrote,

> There is no individual of a company, scarcely excepting the captain himself, on whom more depends for its discipline, police, instruction, and general well being, than on the first sergeant. This is a grade replete with cares and with responsibility. Its duties place its incumbent in constant and direct contact with the men, exercising over them an influence the more powerful as it is immediate and personal; and all experience demonstrates that the condition of every company will improve or deteriorate nearly in proportion to the ability and worth of its first sergeant.[1]

I couldn't help but think of my own mother as I read that description. In my house, the general well-being of our family certainly fell on my mother's shoulders. We depended on her to keep life spinning without too much disruption. She disciplined us, policed us, instructed us, and had more influence on us than anyone else in our formative years. She was the first person we saw in the morning and the last person we saw at night. My brothers and I gave her a run for her money, but she stuck to her guns. Her presence in our lives was something we came to appreciate and respect. I don't know if she ever thought of herself as a first sergeant or if she ever stopped to consider the war she was in, but I know she fought like she understood the importance of her role.

You may not feel your role as mother is important or that anyone sees the tireless hours you put into the lives of your children. Many duties in a mother's life are mundane and routine. But the power, opportunity, and influence you have over the lives of your children can never be underestimated. What is true of a first sergeant is true of a mother: the condition of every child will improve or deteriorate in proportion to the ability and worth of his mother.

The Creed

The Air Force first sergeant's creed is an inspiring summary of his duties:

The Air Force First Sergeant's Creed

I am a First Sergeant.
My job is people—Everyone is my business.
I dedicate my time and energy to their needs;
Their health, morale, discipline, and welfare.
I grow in strength by strengthening my people.
My job is done in faith;
My people build my faith.
The Air Force is my life;
I share it with my people.
I believe in the Air Force goal—
"We take care of our own."
My job is people—
EVERYONE IS MY BUSINESS.

I thought I would make a few changes to this creed and make it applicable to mothers.

The Mother's Creed

My job is my children—
Each one of them is my business.
I dedicate my time and energy to their needs:
Their health, morale, discipline, and welfare.
I love them and I grow in strength by strengthening them.
My job is done in faith;
My children build faith.

Being a parent in today's society is work, and it takes faith and perseverance. It requires the attitude of a first sergeant in the midst of the battle. On the battlefield a first sergeant's main concern is each individual under his care. He makes sure they are eating well and that they are not sick or injured. It is his job to make sure they are physically and mentally ready to fight each and every day. He does not lead the troops out to battle but follows behind to take care of each crisis that might arise. His eyes are on his soldiers. When a soldier is struggling he is there to help. The first sergeant is not focused on the enemy but on making sure that each of his soldiers survives. He is there to make sure they are successful on the battlefield.

Your role as mother is much the same. Your focus is not on the enemy but on your children. It's your job to make sure they have all the tools necessary to be successful on the battlefield. Your job is to focus on the individual needs of your children so they can face the enemy themselves. If our children stand a chance, it is time we lace up the combat boots and realize this is war. Satan is the ultimate adversary, and our children are what we stand to lose.

Chapter 2

Basic Training

Getting Personally Prepared

Before any soldier can hit the battlefield, he must prepare. Basic training is a special program the military designed to train their new recruits for war. I have never been to boot camp, as it is affectionately called, but I have friends who have.

My friends told me a lot of crazy stories about boot camp. Many told me of wild-eyed drill instructors and early morning runs. Basic training is not about meeting new people and building great friendships; it is about survival, surrender, strength, and spirit. Almost everyone I talked with grimaced when they recalled the physical and emotional demands on their bodies and minds. Some said they loved it, some said they hated it, but every single one of them said it was absolutely necessary. When their lives were on the line and their endurance was being tested on the field of battle, they were thankful for that wild-eyed drill instructor who pushed them further than they thought was possible.

As I listened to their stories and thought about the importance of basic training, a simple thought hit me. Every one of those drill instructors had been a new recruit at one point. They had prepared, and now they were preparing others. They pushed the new recruits because they knew how important obedience, respect, discipline, and preparation would be for the survival of each of those soldiers.

So travel back with me in time, back when you were a new recruit. And let's see what we can learn about getting personally prepared.

Remembering Our Childhood

An important tool in personal preparation is remembering. We were all children once, and if we think back, a flood of memories will remind us what those days were like. Do you remember what it was like to wake up and find a pimple on the end of your nose and contemplate faking the flu so you wouldn't have to go to school that day? Do you remember hiding something from your parents and hoping they would never find out? Do you remember your favorite Christmas?

If your memories have gone stale, maybe you could rummage through your old high school yearbooks and look up the things people wrote about you. Dig through boxes, find old diaries and photos, and stir up some stories. Look for the thoughts and feelings you struggled with; ponder the difficulties you encountered in childhood and adolescence.

Sometimes we forget our childhood and can only see the world through adult eyes. We forget all the challenges of childhood because they seem so simple compared to the challenges of adulthood. Taking a walk back through time will remind you of how you once felt about life and give you new insight into your children. It's impossible to anticipate everything your child will face, but remembering what it is like to be her age is a good place to start your preparation.

Lessons from the Past

Now that we've spent time remembering our own childhoods, let's take a look at our original drill sergeants: Mom and Dad.

Parenting is a learned behavior; we tend to follow the same styles of parenting that our parents employed. Despite our best efforts, we catch ourselves saying some of the same phrases that our parents used on us. We copy what we know.

Whether good or bad, your parenting style is a direct result of the way your parents raised you. You either admire your parents' ability and try to copy it or you disagree with the way they handled things and tend to do the opposite. Either way, they influenced you.

I talk to so many women who believe they cannot be good mothers because they did not have a good example to follow. Some were raised in a wonderful home with great parents who set a great example to follow. But having a good role model is not a requirement for being a good parent. Regardless of your upbringing, you can be a wonderful mother who makes a difference in the lives of her children. All mothers must rely on God to give them wisdom and show them which way is right. God will never fail us. He can give us wisdom beyond our years and beyond our background if we just ask. "But if any of you lacks wisdom, let him ask of God, who gives to all generously and without reproach, and it will be given to him" (James 1:5 NASB).

Examine Yourself First

The first place to ask for wisdom is in the area of self-knowledge. Do you love your children enough to examine your own life first? Are you willing to allow God to search your heart and mind and work on the areas He shows you?

We will not be equipped to help our children deal with the smallest of problems if we have huge problems in our own lives. That is why it is so important for you to take the time to examine yourself. Your children will not obey someone they do not respect. They will not listen to your words if your life does not support those words.

Josh Billings was an author and humorist. He wrote after the time of the great Mark Twain and although he never achieved Twain's fame, he was considered by many to be Twain's equal. When writing on parenting Billings had this to say, "To bring up a child in the way he should go, travel that way yourself once in a while."

As a mother it will be necessary for you to make sure you are ready first. Your attitude and personal preparation are necessary if you are going to make a difference in the lives of your children. This is not a "do as I say, not as I do" job. It will never work that way. You have to be confident enough to say, "Follow me as I follow Christ."

There are several ways that you can make sure you are personally ready to lead.

Get Honest, Real Honest

I can't tell you the number of times I have talked with young people who have no confidence in their parents. It's the same story over and over.

"Mom has everyone at church fooled. They think she is really nice but if they could see how she screams at us and throws things at Dad they would think differently."

"Mom is a liar. She lies to everyone including Dad. She has even lied to me several times. I can't trust her."

"Mom doesn't have time for me. Since the divorce, all she has time for is her new boyfriend. She says she loves me but she is never around when I need her."

Your children watch you and they count on you to be honest, consistent, and real. They know you are not perfect, so they need an apology when you lose it. They need to see you are in control of your own emotions so they can trust you with theirs. They need to know that when you talk about Jesus, you do so because you have a real relationship with Him that affects your life.

Before you can be effective in the battle for your children, it's imperative that you prepare yourself spiritually, mentally, and physically. This is never easy for any of us because it requires discipline and dedication. We can find a million excuses why it's too hard. But when it comes down to it, honesty is where we must begin. Knowing my own shortcomings and taking a hard look at my own sin is the first step to victory. Confessing those sins to God and asking for His forgiveness frees up my heart and life to be filled with His power.

Playing church will never give you power. You can go through the motions and you may fool the pastor and every church member, but you can't fool your kids. They know when you are the same person at church and at home. They know when your life matches your words. Nothing is more disillusioning for a child than to have a parent who pretends to be someone she isn't. When this happens, young people lose more than just confidence in their parent; they lose trust for those who claim to know Christ, and they lose faith in the Bible and in God.

Don't give in to the pressure to perform or pretend, for you do not have to be a perfect woman or mother. You will make mistakes, you will say things you regret, you will lose control and behave in ways that are unpleasing to the Lord. But when you do, you must ask for forgiveness quickly, and work on changing your behavior. Let your children know they have a mother who is willing to admit her mistakes and deal with them. They will respect you for that and follow your lead.

Don't pretend that you have it all together. I can think of nothing that inhibits communication between children and their parents more than this obstacle. If they don't feel you can relate to real life then they will not come to you for counsel. If they watch you pretend your life is always great then they assume they must do the same.

I am not advising you to share all your mistakes with your children, but they should know that their mom is what she is by the grace of God. They should know that your life stinks sometimes too and that it's okay to cry. They should hear you pray and ask God to supply your needs. Our children learn so much about God when they watch us walk with Him in good times and bad.

Two Key Disciplines

A key aspect of boot camp is obedience in the daily routines. If a recruit cannot follow simple orders to make his bed, to groom himself, or to stand at attention, he is much less likely to obey orders given in the heat of battle. In other words, if the recruit does not learn to exercise discipline in small tasks, he is likely to fail to exercise discipline in the larger tasks given to him.

I grew up in church and in a wonderful Christian home, where I learned two daily disciplines that are key to the Christian walk: prayer and Bible reading. As a young person I struggled to incorporate these disciplines into my life. I would do well for a while and then slack off.

But as I grew older, God began to show me that these were more than just disciplines to be acquired; they were my access to a personal relationship with Him. When I realized that God wanted to talk to me personally through His Word and that I could pour my heart out to Him in prayer, these portals of communication took on new life for me. I wasn't just reading my Bible to check off a list; I needed to hear what God wanted to tell me. I also needed His wisdom and direction in my life. God's Word says wisdom is available to anyone who asks, and so I began to ask in prayer and receive in the Word. It was amazing how God began to change my life. What was once a ritual became an exciting personal relationship. God's Word began to do its work in my heart and life, and I began to grow like never before.

I meet so many people who, like me, have spent many years going through the motions and doing a poor job of it. In order to be prepared for what life throws at you, your faith must be more than ritual; it has to be relationship.

Personally, where are you? What is your time with God like? I am not asking you if you read your Bible every day or if you read all of it in a year. I am asking if you are getting something personal from God when you read it. Is He speaking to you? How about your time in conversation with Him? Are you real with Him, or do you spend your time spouting off a bunch of phrases that have no meaning so that you can say you prayed?

It's a battle out there; this is no time for playing games. If you are not where you need to be with God, how can you lead your children? If your faith is not real for you, why do you expect them to take it seriously? You will earn the respect of your children when they see a real person in a real relationship with Jesus Christ. They may not appreciate your rules or agree with your strategies, but they will respect your walk.

What is so amazing about our intimate relationship with God is what it prepares us for and what it gives us power to do. In ourselves we have no power or foresight. But God knows the steps ahead and the obstacles that we will face. He has promised that He will never place anything on us that is too hard for us to bear (1 Corinthians 10:13).

God also promises that if we yoke our lives to Him, He will make our load light and easy (Matthew 11:29–30). You are not in this alone; God is with you. He has chosen to place His strength beside your weakness and pull along with you. Even if you are a single parent, you are not in this alone. God has promised to come alongside you and do what you cannot do.

You require God's power and wisdom to be the parent that your children need. So how's your relationship? Are you engaging in the two key disciplines: prayer and Bible reading?

Preparing to Teach

I used to tell my college students that there was one sure way to know whether they were ready for a test—if they could put the terms and concepts in their own words and teach it to someone else. It's almost impossible to formulate ideas into your own words if you do not understand the ideas first.

The same is true when teaching your children. In order to prepare a child biblically for the task ahead of him we must first make sure *we* can pass the test. There is a great passage of Scripture that explains this concept beautifully:

> Likewise urge the young men to be sensible; *in all things show your-self to be an example of good deeds*, with purity in doctrine, dignified, sound in speech which is beyond reproach, so that the opponent will be put to shame, having nothing bad to say about us. (Titus 2:6–8 NASB, emphasis mine)

As parents we need to live by biblical guidelines so that we can teach them to our younger ones. The progression is easy to spot—you live it first; you teach it second.

So how then are we to live? In Titus 2:2–5 Paul clearly lists character traits that are important in every good representative of Christ:

temperate	pure
dignified	sober
sensible	hard-working
sound in faith	kind
loving	good teachers
able to endure	encouragers
reverent	

This is a pretty extensive and challenging list. But I don't think it is a mistake that Christ wants us to *live* these traits so that we can *teach* these traits. Our lives say a lot about our relationship with Jesus Christ. Young people have a keen eye for spotting fakes. They recognize when we are saying words that do not match up with our daily lives. We must prepare to teach our children by living out those teachings in our lives. God doesn't want us to teach our children a list of do's and don'ts that have no meaning to them.

The gospel was given to all of us, without cost or condition. However, after we are saved, God asks us to lay our lives on the altar as living sacrifices (Romans 12:1–2), dying daily to our self-will. This is where relationship and communion with God begins.

Please don't misunderstand me; I am not minimizing salvation but rather stressing that salvation is only the beginning. God desires to have a personal, intimate relationship with us, His children. Salvation opens the door for this relationship to take place, and sanctification is the process by which we are changed into His image. So this list in Titus is not just a set of rules and regulations that are required of us; they are the descriptors of someone who is walking intimately with her Lord.

Take the time right now to look in the mirror of the Word of God and be honest about what you see. Does this passage describe your life? Are you sound in faith? Are you loving and kind? Are you worthy of respect?

It is important that you evaluate yourself before you start teaching your children. As God reveals your areas of weakness to you, get on your face before Him. He is loving and gracious, and He will help you get your own life in order.

Are You Prepared?

In the boot camp of life, every mother is a drill instructor. As a mother, it's your job to instill obedience, respect, and discipline into your children's character so they are prepared for whatever life throws at them. If you don't prepare them for life, who will?

But before you drill your children, ask yourself: Have I successfully completed spiritual boot camp? Have I faced up to and dealt with my own problems? Am I honest about myself? Do I live my life the same way at home as I do at church or out in the world? Do I read my Bible, pray, and seek God's leading in my daily life? Does my life exhibit the character traits of someone who is strong in faith?

Am *I* personally prepared?

Chapter 3

Attention!

Are You Connecting?

One of the first things a person learns when entering the military is how to stand at attention. Attention is about discipline, respect, and honor. It's about listening and learning from someone who has your best interests at heart. The military knows something that mothers need to know: if you are going to make a lasting impact on someone, you must get their attention.

I am not asking you to line your children up at 6:00 a.m. or enforce your commands with push-ups. The military has its ways of getting attention from the men and women who don the uniform, but as a mother you must have your own strategies. Getting your child's attention is more than just getting her to listen to you when you talk. You gain your child's attention by connecting deeply with her. And you must connect with your children at a deeper level than anything else can reach: deeper than friends, deeper than any media, deeper than the wiles of the devil.

Getting Their Attention

I am not sure what is more difficult: teaching children to give appropriate attention or getting their attention so you can teach them. The competition for your child's attention is staggering, and it starts when they're very young. Cartoons and video games capture the youngest of children and begin to shape the way they think. The older they become, the louder and more technical the competition becomes. As your children grow older it will take great effort to get their attention and much more to keep it.

Sometimes as adults we feel left behind and out of touch with what our kids know and what they are experiencing. Today even preschoolers can operate a computer. Seventh graders are teaching us how to send e-mail or surf the Internet. Teenagers carry cell phones and ask for the latest MP3 players. And using only their thumbs, college freshmen can text at the speed of sound. Most anything is just a keystroke away in today's fast-paced, high-tech world.

Our children have seen more and experienced more before they turn thirteen than many of their grandparents did in their entire life. But most of the things they are experiencing are simulated. Although they have seen graphic images of war on the nightly news, very few have ever fought for their country or for their lives like their grandfathers did. They are maturing in a society that works less, consumes more, and appreciates little. Everything is bigger, better, and brighter than ever before, and for only a few extra dollars it can surround you on all sides.

But with all this technology comes a certain staleness and coldness. Now we have speed dating, practice marriages, and the pace at which we are moving is only getting faster, leaving no time for what really matters: relationships. Relationships take work and time. They are not built from five-minute conversations on the way to soccer practice or while you are waiting for the computer to boot up. They take a stillness that is not common or comfortable to this society. And relationships take commitment, a word that has for all practical purposes been removed from our vocabulary.

As a mother, you must commit your love and a significant amount of time if you want to connect with your children and capture their attention.

A Mother's Love

The first and most crucial ingredient to gaining your child's attention is love. In many ways, maternal love is instinctive. Brenda Hunter describes the special nature of this love beautifully:

When a woman becomes a mother, she begins an inner journey that revolutionizes her life. She begins a journey to her heart. Because of her children's love, neediness, and daily demands, she can no longer simply think of herself: her body, her success, her marriage, and her future. She must make room in her heart and life for another person. In so doing, a woman is transformed. She in turn, profoundly shapes her children's sense of self, values, conscience, and capacity for empathy and intimacy—the core of all that makes them human. A mother touches her children's very souls. Such is the radiant, life-changing power of mother love.[2]

Poems, songs, and countless tributes have been written about the love of a mother and her influence in her children's lives. Some of the most successful people in the entire world have directly linked their success to the influence of their mothers. Two of our country's greatest presidents gave powerful accolades to their mothers. Abraham Lincoln said, "All that I am or ever hope to be, I owe to my angel mother." George Washington said, "All I am I owe to my mother. I attribute all my success in life to the moral, intellectual and physical education I received from her."

A mother begins with an *instinctive* love, but the more precious and enduring *unconditional* love is honed over many years of practice. Being a mother who loves her children biblically is a challenging feat. It requires a balance of love and acceptance with judgment and consequence. It seamlessly weaves freedom and responsibility together to produce a wise steward who enjoys the goodness of God.

A mother is a teacher, a mentor, and a guide as well as a friend, a comforter, and a cheerleader. A mother shows love through more than just words. Mothers touch, they hug, they cheer. They cry, they pray, they believe. Mothers have an amazing way of communicating confidence, strength, value, and worth to their children through the love they give. When a child knows that she is loved unconditionally, the foundation for greatness has been set.

Gary Chapman wrote a wonderful book entitled *The Five Love Languages*. In this book he demonstrates that all of us have a way that we receive love best. Most of the time the way we like to receive love is also the way we give love. We tend to project our values and desires on others. In doing this we support our own feelings about life and love. Read this book and figure out what your children's love languages are, then show them love in a way that allows them to *feel* that love. And accept your children as they are, no strings attached.

The Gift of Time

The second crucial ingredient for gaining your children's attention is time. There are many ways to show children that you love them, but one of the greatest is the gift of your time. Spending time with your children lets them know they are important to you. Take time to play with them or to read a story together. Attend their ballgames and events. Make them a priority in your life.

As you give your children your time, they begin to understand that you appreciate them and they are valuable to you. When you stop doing something important to be with them it says, "You are important to me, more important than what I was doing." Our children need to know that out of all the things that we have going on in our lives, they are at the top of the list.

Making people feel important is often an inconvenience because we are almost always in the middle of something. Sure, there are times when you really can't stop what you are doing, and your child needs to know that he will have to wait. But there are so many times when we could stop if we wanted to. The problem is that we don't want to stop. We don't want to be bothered. Children notice, and after a while they quit asking.

Too Busy to Invest in Your Children?

One of the biggest challenges that women talk to me about is how busy they are. They are overwhelmed with the pace of life and concerned that there is no time left to really invest in the lives of their children. One mother commented to me that out of everyone involved in her daughter's daily life, she and her husband were the ones who saw her the least.

God has given parents the responsibility to raise their children the right way. Biblical child training is a process that takes time and patience. In the average home today both parents work. For many, dual incomes are necessary for survival, but this makes it very difficult to spend quality, training time with children. By the time everyone gets home from work and school, there is just enough time to eat a quick supper and start homework and baths. The last thing an exhausted mom is thinking of is her children's different characteristics and how they can best be trained.

After a hard day, you feel fortunate if your children get their homework done quickly and race to the television for their favorite show. At least they are occupied and quiet for a few hours. By the time the kitchen is cleaned up and a load of laundry has been washed, it is time to start putting the youngest to bed. A quick hug and kiss at the end of the bedtime story and on to the next task. As you fall into bed, reviewing your schedule for tomorrow, you wonder why your teenager hides away in his room all night and your ten-year-old seems exceptionally quiet lately. But you don't have the time or the energy to deal with it right now, maybe tomorrow.

Unfortunately, this is a common scene in the average home. Mothers sense when things are not quite right with their children, but many don't seem to have the time or energy to deal with the nudges they are getting in their hearts. So how do we stop the madness? How do we take back the time with our children that is being stolen from us every day?

The first place to start is with you. Every mother reading this book should analyze why you need to work. And before you say to pay the bills, evaluate your lifestyle! Could you do without a few gadgets, buy used cars instead of new ones, and cut back a little here and there to stay home? The question is, do you have to work to make it, or do you work to live at the level to which you have become accustomed? Are those nice things and vacations more important to you than your children? If you knew that cutting back on your hours so you could be home when school got out would make a difference in your child's future, would you do it? If you knew that staying home with those little ones would save them heartache and pain, would you do it? Pray and ask God to lead and guide your family in this area. If you have no option but to work outside the home, then your plate will be full, but God will give you the strength to manage your load.

We parents must take responsibility, for we set the example for our children to follow. The home atmosphere is created by the parents first. According to most studies, the average parent spends much less time with their children than their parents spent with them. Years ago we were a more rural society and families worked and played together. This gave parents a lot more time with their children. Then society shifted to the suburban lifestyle and our lives became mobile. Lifestyle changes have eaten away at the time we actually spend with our children. What once was three to four hours a day has turned into fifteen minutes a day. In fact, Josh McDowell reports that out of those fifteen minutes, twelve minutes are spent in criticism or instruction. This leaves only about three minutes a day in meaningful conversation.[3]

Quality Comes from Quantity

Parents must carve out family time and make it a sacred appointment. *Quality* time will come only as we spend *quantity* time with our children. There are some moments that you just can't schedule. Important conversations that you need to have with your children require good timing. Teachable moments are created in the flow of life. Moms have to make sure they are in the same flow of life as their children if they are going to find these moments.

In my former role as dean of women for a Christian college, I spent many hours talking to girls about tough situations in their lives. For five years many girls came to my office to talk. In almost every session I would ask one simple question: "Can you talk to your mother?" The majority of young ladies said, "No, not about stuff like this." When I asked them why, their answers varied, but one answer kept coming up over and over: "I don't have that kind of relationship with my mom." If that is true, then mothers must work hard to form the kind of relationship with their daughters that can handle tough conversations and can provide a place of safety and trust.

If you are a mother of a teenager, listen carefully. Teenagers need their parents. The adolescent years are filled with many ups and downs, and the number of changes children go through in the process of becoming adults is staggering. True, they have their own schedules and friends, and it's hard to get in their lives and spend time, but just because it's hard doesn't mean it's not necessary. As they process many new ideas and concepts, you must be there to provide guidance and support. When children become teens the strategies may change, but you still must make the effort to be a part of their lives. If not, you will lose *their* attention by *your* lack of attention.

It's time to rethink and reorganize. What could you change or eliminate in your schedule so you could spend more time with your children? What consumes you so much that you can't put it down or stop for ten minutes? Ask yourself if it's that important. When was the last time you had one-on-one time with your children? When was the last time you just did something fun with them for no reason? If you are struggling to know where to begin, let me give you some tips that might get you started.

Family Dinner

Sit down for dinner at least one night a week with the entire family. Notice I didn't say what the meal had to be; just make sure you are all sitting down together at a table.

Family Moment

Have a family moment every day. Sometimes the best time for this is right before bedtime. Gather everyone around and talk for a few moments. You might decide to purchase a family devotional and read something from it or just have everyone share a special thought. This is not a time for discipline or tattling on each other; it should be a moment of togetherness. Conclude your time by praying together.

The One-Minute Prayer

Before your children leave for school every morning, touch them and say a brief prayer for them. Or if you take them to school, use the commute time to get specific prayer requests from them, and then say a quick prayer together before you drop them off.

The Prayer Huddle

Anytime there is an urgent need or an important issue that needs to be prayed for, bring the family together. Huddle everyone up close and pick one or two people to pray for that need. When God answers that prayer, make sure you have a "praise huddle" to thank Him for His goodness.

One on One

Find one time each week to do something with each of your children. Some weeks it could be a big deal and take several hours; other times it could just be a simple twenty-minute activity. Remember this is their time not yours, so do what they like. Color, play a computer game, shoot some hoops, ride a bike, paint your nails. Regardless of what it is, make it special.

Family Nights

At least once a month and more often if possible, clear all schedules for family night. This will take planning, so sit down with your calendar ahead of time and clearly mark the night. Then make sure everyone knows this is a "no miss" event. Make it fun! Get everyone involved, regardless of their age. Get ideas from your children.

GLUE Meetings

GLUE stand stands for Give, Love, Understand, Expect. Everyone needs to understand these simple truths if the family is going to hold together. Each member of your family must give sacrificially, love unconditionally, understand another person's perspective, and expect the best of themselves and each other. GLUE meetings are times when the whole family is called into conference because something is pulling the family apart or something is needed to push the family closer together.

These meetings don't always have to be negative, but sometimes things go wrong that affect the entire family. A GLUE meeting is a great place to discuss these issues openly and honestly. Sometimes one person's bad decision affected others and a public apology needs to be made to the family so the relationships can be restored. But a GLUE meeting is also a great place to discuss family vacations and other fun activities. As your children get older, explain that anyone in the family can call a meeting as long as they have gotten approval from both parents.

A word of caution: GLUE meetings should not be called for anything and everything. If that happens, they lose their importance. Make sure you think through the necessity of calling everyone together. If it didn't start with everyone, it probably doesn't need to end with everyone. Also never use a GLUE meeting to embarrass or single out anyone. Remember, this time is about drawing closer as a family.

Monitor Your Child's Time

Mothers are responsible for helping their children see the value of time. Many mothers are so concerned about their children being popular or successful that they encourage them to fill their lives with activities. Sports, music, and youth group are all worthwhile—just make sure you leave room for family time as well.

I grew up playing sports. In the fall I played volleyball, in the winter it was basketball, and in the spring it was softball. I was on the varsity team in all three sports by the eighth grade, so juggling my schoolwork and athletics was a full-time job. On some nights pizza or McDonald's was about the best we could do, but in the midst of all that activity, my parents kept my brothers and me anchored to the things that mattered. They stressed the importance of balance and priorities. They guarded our schedules but gave us freedom to make decisions regarding how we spent our time. From their teaching and example I learned the importance of time management and the necessity of saying "no." I learned when I give someone my undivided attention I am showing them respect and worth. I am forever indebted to my parents for all the time and attention they gave me.

Our fast-paced busyness is being passed on to our children. They watch as their parents dash from one thing to the next, and they follow suit. As parents practice this juggling act of time and attention in their own lives, they begin to teach their children how to juggle them as well.

Get Attention by Giving Attention

What will it take to get your child's attention? Give her yours! Start with a decision to make your children a priority in your life. It's more than just running her to all her events. It's more than buying her the latest fashions so she can be accepted. It's being there, heart, mind, and soul. Even cooking meals and washing clothes cannot substitute for focused attention.

Recently I saw a mother going into the grocery store with her nine- or ten-year-old daughter in tow. She hustled across the parking lot toward the front doors, never looking back to see if her daughter was looking for cars or close behind. I thought, *Surely this can't be the girl's mother* as I looked both ways for traffic. But I was wrong. The girl made a feeble attempt to catch up by squeaking out, "Mom, wait on me." The mother never turned around.

The little girl finally caught up to her mom as they were entering the store. She reached out to take her mom's swinging hand but she was just out of reach and missed it. Her mom picked up her pace as she grabbed a shopping cart and rolled it into the store never noticing her daughter's presence. I smiled at the young girl as we entered the second set of doors together. She sighed and looked down at the ground as she hustled to keep up.

As I moved through the store grabbing the few things I needed from the shelves, I couldn't get that little girl off my mind. I walked to the checkout area and saw her in the distance. She was still dragging behind her mom, staring at the ground.

Maybe the mom was under great duress and this was not her usual manner. Maybe the little girl had been a real pain to deal with before they got to the store and the mom had taken all she was going to take that day. I don't know for sure, but what I do know is that mother is missing out on moments she will never get back. I couldn't help but wonder how she got so self-absorbed. What could be so important that you would ignore your daughter's cry to be with you?

Sadly enough that little girl won't be little much longer. She will not always reach up for her mom's hand. I wanted to run over to that lady and shake her. I wanted to show her a videotape of her actions. I wanted to show her what she had missed. But instead I grabbed my stuff and headed out to my car.

I do live in reality. I too can be self-absorbed and in too much of a hurry. And I am not trying to make you feel guilty and over-whelmed. I know that being a mother may just be the toughest job on earth. But I also think it just might be the most rewarding job on earth. Your children need you. They need you for more than what you *do* for them. They need you to *be* for them. So if you want to get their attention, give them some first.

Chapter 4

Attention, Part Two

Are You Communicating?

All of us are familiar with this stereotypical scene: a sergeant gets up in the face of a misbehaving soldier and yells at him, while the soldier stands at attention, unblinking. As a child one of my favorite shows was *Gomer Pyle, U.S.M.C.* I used to laugh hysterically as Gomer, the goofy private, infuriated Sergeant Carter. It seemed Gomer could never quite get things right, and the Sergeant was always red in the face and nose-to-nose with him as he corrected his behavior. Gomer always just stood there and took it with that goofy look on his face.

Sometimes this looks like the picture of our parenting communication style. We yell. Our kids just stand there. We yell louder. They smirk and still do nothing. A bystander might observe that we are communicating at least according to one definition of the word: we are making something known by clear signs. But a richer form of communication contains the idea of "communing"—talking over, discussing, connecting intimately. It is that second, richer form of communication I want to discuss here.

Too many of us focus on the *talking* side of communication. But we can talk to our children until we are blue in the face and they will continue to tune us out unless we first model a crucial aspect of communication: *listening.*

Be a Listener

Several months ago I was at my daughter's house. Brandi has four wonderful boys, and when I am around they all want Nana's attention. On this particular day I was trying to have a conversation with Brandi and play with the boys at the same time. Luke, who is a delightful four-year-old, was finally tired of me not giving him my undivided attention. He crawled into my lap, put both of his hands on the sides of my face, and pulled my face around until I was nose-to-nose with him. Then looking me directly in the eye he said, "Nana, I am trying to tell you something very important and you are not listening to me. Try to focus, okay?" I couldn't help but smile and give him my undivided attention for the next few minutes. And just as fast as he had come, he was gone, off to play with his brothers.

This little incident illustrates three very concrete, active, even physical ways of showing that you want to be a good listener: (1) stop what you're doing, (2) use body language, and (3) hear them out.

Stop What You're Doing!

So many times kids don't want an hour or even twenty minutes—they just have something they need to share, and if you will take the time to stop, look, and listen, *you* will be the one who gets to hear their heart. As much as possible, when your child wants your attention, stop what you're doing and give it. If you train yourself to pay attention early in his life, you will be ready to listen and pay attention when he enters the teenage years.

I know when children are young, mothers are faced with stimulus overload. They are constantly hearing their name called and they are asked to respond to a thousand questions. It is easy to begin to tune your children out so that you can get some peace or get something done. Mothers multitask all the time: they cook a meal, help with homework, and fix a broken toy all in a matter of minutes. This is why it is so important that mothers don't develop bad habits in the area of listening to their children.

Hearing your children and *listening* to them are two very different things. When they are small they can drive you crazy with all their ceaseless chatter. But as they began to mature it is so very important that you give them your focused attention as a listener. Actively listening to what your young person is saying is crucial for keeping the doors of communication open between the two of you. And the first step in active listening is to *stop what you're doing.* Or if you cannot stop, at least acknowledge your child's need, let him know when you will attend to him, and follow up on your promise. Simply stopping and listening may be difficult at times, but in the end it will enable you to prevent problems and guide your children to better problem-solving skills.

Use Body Language

When you really listen to your child, you communicate that with your body language. After you stop what you are doing, get close to her and look her in the eyes. Don't interrupt her or interject your opinion too early; let her talk. She will learn that she can come to you with things she feels are important and you will take the time to hear her out.

Hear Them Out

Opening the communication door at an early age is an important step in keeping it open as kids grow older. So many parents complain about the fact that they can't get their teen to open up to them, but many have never made it a habit to listen, and their teenager knows it.

Teenagers enjoy talking about themselves. They will blog about their deepest feelings and emotions for the entire world to see, but they feel overwhelmed if they think their parents might read it. When I've asked teens about why they weren't comfortable discussing their feelings with their parents, it became clear that in many cases parents had closed the door of communication by their words and actions.

Children ask tough questions. They make statements to get a response. They act as if they are uninterested. But these are all feelers to see how their parents will respond. They evaluate first, communicate second. They are worried they are going to look stupid or sound dumb. They are nervous the listener is going to laugh at them or ridicule them. So they test the waters before diving in. They throw out shocking statements to test the freak-out factor, or they give the friend scenario to test the understanding factor.

As a mother you have to choose your words wisely. Think about positive comments that will help your child continue to talk to you. You want your children to know that you are interested in what they are saying. In order to understand what they are thinking, you will need to listen to everything they want to say. Be patient with them as they grope to find the right words. Be careful not to say things that will shut down communication. Phrases like "You don't need to know about that" or "We don't talk about things like that" will cause your child to stop talking.

Don't Freak Out!

Moms can unknowingly send the wrong signals, because their facial expressions and voice levels send strong messages to their children. These nonverbal communications can indicate an altogether different message than the one you are trying to send. As I talk to teenage girls, I ask them why they don't feel they can talk to their mothers. The number one reason I receive is, "She would freak out!" When I ask them why they think their mother would freak out if they have never tried to talk to her about these issues before, their answer is almost always unanimous: "She does it all the time, over hardly anything, no way am I talking to her about this."

Recognize yourself? Oh, I know it is a scary world out there. It is definitely enough to give the average parent a nervous breakdown. But your children need to know there is a safe haven where they can go and talk about difficult issues. If they are ever going to be able to do this you have to learn to check your emotions at the door. Nothing could be more heartbreaking than finally getting your children to open up and actually talk about important issues and then watch them shut down because you went into hysterics. As a woman you are more prone to show your emotions, but it is vital that you stay in control. "Freaking out," as your children call it, is a sure way to send them scurrying away.

Convey the right signals to your children. Learn to smile first. A gentle smile conveys that you heard them and that they are not in trouble for what they said. Second, take a deep breath as you are smiling. This will help to calm your nerves and will give you a second to focus. If the question is one that should be answered in a private setting, quietly let him know that you will talk about it when the two of you are alone.

Once you are at a location where you can talk, allow your child to talk openly about what is on his mind. No matter how strong you feel the need to stop him and straighten him out—don't! Wait until he is through talking. Pray and ask God to give you wisdom as he speaks. Listen to *everything* he has to say. Many times we get so hung up on the first thing that blew us out of the water that we never hear our child's whole heart. Your child will often surprise you with his maturity and good judgment if you take the time to listen for it.

Finally, keep your voice under control. Your tone and pitch have so much to do with your ability to correctly communicate your heart. If you are loud and shrieking it indicates panic and will send your listener into stress, which will close him down. If you keep your voice even and steady, your listener will relax and open up more. Breathing, smiling, listening, and a steady calm voice will help send the right signals to your child. You can run into your room and scream into your pillow after it's over if necessary.

Once your children realize that you will listen to them and give them a chance to communicate in an honest and respectful manner, the doors will open. Yes, they will keep certain things to themselves, but as a general rule they will come to you because they know you will listen. As you demonstrate through your own life what it means to be a good listener, you can look forward to them returning the favor. Expect them to listen to you with the same patience and respect that you give them.

Start Talking

Now that we've covered the basics of good listening, I want to encourage you to start talking. Because, believe it or not, I've also found that a parent *not talking* can cause as much trouble as a parent talking too much!

Even before birth mothers talk to their children. They sing to them, read to them, and continually chatter with them as if they can completely understand. So why do we clam up when it comes to the conversations that are really important? Parents *must* become the source of truth for their young people. The world is coming at them from every angle with flashy, over-the-top messages. The colors are bright, the music is loud, and the graphics are amazing, but there is very little truth in what is being told. There doesn't have to be any truth; all that matters out in the world is what sells.

If you are going to prepare your children, you have to get involved. You'll never make a difference standing on the outside of their lives. Mothers of toddlers might feel as if they have plenty of time; they don't. Now is the time to start. Some of you have preteens and teens and you know how accelerated things become when they hit this age. Regardless of your child's age, it's never too late to start talking to them about the important issues.

Most parents start out in the center of their children's lives, but as their children grow older it's easy to get kicked to the outer edges. Learning to communicate with your children is one of the most important things you can do to get in, stay in, and make an impact.

Keep Their Age, Maturity, and Environment in Mind

As children develop they are naturally curious about life and what makes things tick. They ask hundreds of questions and touch, taste, and smell a variety of things along the way. They want to learn. Instead of squelching this curiosity, mothers should fan the flame with the right information at the right time. The idea that one day when your child is old enough you will sit down with her and have this big talk is really not the approach to take. Learning should come as a process. All along the way you should listen for the cues that your children are giving you and take those opportunities to talk to them about any number of issues.

Simple answers to their questions are usually the best way to start. Listen to their conversations about different aspects of life and find your opportunity to jump in and establish truth. As they grow their questions will become more complex, and your answers will need to match their maturity.

I have known many parents who did not realize how much exposure their children were getting at such an early age. Your child's environment may dictate the necessity of having certain conversations earlier than you would prefer. As your children interact with other children they will pick up on terms and information. This is why it is vital that your voice be heard. You must prepare them for the things they will hear as they go to school, watch television, listen to music, and interact with others. They must know the correct information, and they need to hear it from you.

If you start this process early, you will have a better prospect of discussing the difficult issues with your teens. Teens do not always ask questions, so it will be important for you to lay a foundation for this type of dialogue at a young age.

Lead by Example

Communication and attention start with you. Mothers set the tone in so many households. Your children are counting on you to build a meaningful relationship with them. They are counting on you to make a commitment of your time, to have significant conversations with them, and to discover what is happening in their lives. Oh, at times they will roll their eyes and act as if you are killing them, but don't be fooled: they love that you care and that you just want to be with them.

Too many mothers are waiting on their children to lead in this area. You will be waiting a long time if you are waiting on your teenager to lead. Young people love relationships but struggle with how to build healthy ones. Today our young people are constructing relationships in cyberspace. They share their deepest feelings with complete strangers when their own parents have no idea how they feel. Granted some of this is just "teenage stuff" and is to be expected, but I believe that our young people would not be so addicted to texting and blogging if a need was not being met there. So communicate with your child. Give her your undivided attention. Listen without freaking out. And don't be afraid to speak truth into her life.

Chapter 5

Training Soldiers

Preparation Is Protection

The Army has specialized training for soldiers called the Warrior Transition Course that covers everything important to understanding the "Army Way." Trainees are taught about the leadership structure of the Army, teamwork, and drill and ceremony. These skills help every soldier know that he is not alone and that he has a role in making things go smoothly.

During the second week, the soldiers are taken to the firing range, where they must prove they can hit the target in almost any condition. The last two sections of this course, physical fitness and tactical training, are the hardest for most soldiers. Soldiers must demonstrate that they are physically ready for the demands that will be put on them when they face the enemy. During tactical training the setting is modeled directly after the battlefield. Live fire is used, civilians are wandering around the towns, and wrecked vehicles are scattered along the route. It is made to look real and feel real because some day it will be real for many of these soldiers.

Major Ralph Hudnall is the executive officer for the 1st Battalion, 46th Infantry Regiment, which trains these soldiers. He said, "We train these soldiers with the expectation that every single one of them will see combat."[4] Major Hudnall is correct. Fifty percent of their soldiers see combat in the next six months, and within three years all of them have been on the battlefield.

Have you thought about the fact that as a mother you are training soldiers? Are you training them like you expect them to see combat? The battlefield may look very different than that of the Warrior Transition Course, but your children will spend most of their lives on a spiritual battlefield. Temptation is real, sin is everywhere, and the fight for their hearts and lives is fierce. Mothers must prepare them for combat.

The Warrior Transition course is effective because trainees get the chance to train for combat under the guidance and protection of their superior officers. If a trainee makes a mistake, he can do so in a safe environment where he can live and learn from it. As your children grow older, they will need to transition as well. Give them room to test their training while they are still under your protection and guidance. This practice will prepare them for success when they are alone behind enemy lines.

Paul wrote to Timothy shortly before he was martyred. In his last letter to the young man he had mentored in the faith, he wrote these powerful words, "Endure hardness as a good soldier of Jesus Christ" (2 Timothy 2:3–4). Paul goes on to remind Timothy that he is in a battle and cannot afford to get tangled up with the things of this life. He must stay focused on the One who called him to be a soldier. Even though Timothy was just a young man when he met Paul, Paul believed Timothy was ready to be a soldier thanks to the training his mother and grandmother had given him at home.

Can the same be said of you? Are you the kind of mother who is training her children to be good soldiers? Your home is the Warrior Transition Course for your children. There they will learn what they need to fight temptation, to walk in wisdom and discernment, to stand for what is right, to be salt and light in a world with desperate needs, and to endure suffering.

Remember, you are not the only one who desires to influence your children. Recruiters are everywhere, vying for attention and loyalty. They make their world look fun, exciting, and new. They talk a good line and they seem to have the lifestyle to back it up. They use every means of communication to be heard, and their voice is almost impossible to ignore. They target everyone, but they love children because they know if they get them early enough, they usually stay for life. They are deceitful; they are tricksters; they are the enemy. They hate, they destroy, and they don't care.

We can't assume our children aren't listening to these voices. We can't pretend that our children cannot be influenced by their persuasive speech. As a mother, you must *expect* your children to face the enemy, and train them with that in mind. Parents must get on the offensive. They must protect and teach so that when the battles come, their children will be prepared.

From the moment their child is placed in their arms, mothers have a fierce protective instinct. Marketers capitalize on this instinct by selling new mothers numerous gadgets to "baby-proof" their homes. But protection of the wrong sort can actually harm more than it helps.

I want to look at what it means to be a mother who goes on the offense in preparing her children for life. A serious mother will not let anything come in the way of child training. I am afraid so many mothers today are clueless. It's not that they don't love their children, they do. They want them to have the best life can offer, but they have no idea where that philosophy is taking them. It's time that Satan, our enemy, understands that mothers are more than just soft, cuddly, emotional women—they are a force to be reckoned with. For this to happen mothers must take a hard look at their methods.

So how do we protect our children? Before I give the answer, there are two equally dangerous schools of thought on this that I'd like to address: (1) the isolation theory and (2) the existential theory.

The Isolation Theory

The first instinct of a protective parent is to isolate their children from anything that could harm them or influence them in the wrong direction. As parents look around, they see more and more corruption. Fearful parents believe that in order to keep their children free of bad influences, they must keep them out of the world and away from almost every person in it. The theory is, "If my child is isolated, he will not be influenced."

This attempt to build a fort around the lives of their children and keep them from encountering anything that might lead them astray becomes the full-time focus for many parents. They realize the problems with public schools, so they send their children to Christian schools. When they see problems at the Christian school, they decide to home school. They see the influence of their children's friends, so they don't allow them to have many friends. They encourage themselves by making statements that reinforce their theory such as "We don't allow our children to listen to that music" or "Our children are not allowed to date." They feel the further they go with this theory, the safer their children will be.

Now understand, I don't have any problem with home schooling; in fact, in many cases it is the best choice a parent can make. But my question is this: "Why are you home schooling?" If the answer is to keep your children secluded from the world, then I believe your reasoning is unbiblical. And if you actually believe that by not allowing your children to do certain things, you keep them out of danger, you are in for great disappointment. Here again your thinking is unbiblical.

I think it was Mark Twain who said that when children turn twelve we should build a box, put them in it, and cut a hole in the top of the box so they can breathe. Then when they turn sixteen, plug the hole. Of course Mark Twain in his satirical and humorous way was painting a picture of the difficulty in bringing up teens. But for many Christian parents, this "box" idea does not sound like a bad one. Most parents I have talked to are frustrated and fearful concerning their young people. So they create boxes out of their homes and churches. They believe these fortresses will protect their children from all the evil around them.

I talked to one mother recently who assured me her daughter would not have any problems with sex before marriage, lust, or boys in general. I was intrigued at what would give this mother so much confidence, so I asked why she was so sure. She replied, "We don't allow our children to sit with or play with the opposite sex at any time unless they are a relative. Our oldest daughter is twelve now, and she knows any boy other than her brother and father is to be avoided. No boys—no problems."

I know that mother meant well and that she desired to protect her children, but her theory was unbiblical and could cause great grief and pain for her and her daughter in the coming years.

Think about it. If we put our children in a literal box to keep them from getting hurt, we might provide an increased measure of safety, but the cruelty of the prison that we have created would not only get us arrested for child abuse, but would also affect our children in negative ways, regardless of the sincerity of our intentions. If this behavior is considered crazy in the physical sense, can we not also see the absurdity in the emotional, spiritual, and mental sense? Mark Twain's box shows us one thing for sure: it is easier to box your child up than to train him.

Problems with the Isolation Theory

As we are beginning to see, there are several problems with this theory of isolation. First of all, Jesus prayed explicitly to His Father, "I do not ask You to take them out of the world, but to protect them from the evil one" (John 17:15 NASB). God left us here on this earth for the purpose of telling others about Christ. He commands us in the Sermon on the Mount to be salt and light, and in the book of Acts He commands us to go into all the world. But how can we be effective salt if we stay in the shaker, and how can we be effective light if we don't go into the darkness?

One of my favorite summertime meals is fresh corn on the cob. I love to fire up the grill and fix my corn right on the hot coals. Peaches and Cream corn is my absolute favorite. I could actually make a whole meal of just corn. But I have to admit that as much as I love that corn, it's not ready to eat until I add the butter and salt. But what if someone said, "No, you can't put salt on the corn; the salt will get contaminated with butter and corn! Salt must be kept pure, isolated and protected from all foods." Do you see the absurdity of this statement? Never using salt on food actually defeats the whole purpose of salt. Salt is not meant to be kept to itself. It is produced to enhance the flavor of food, to bring out the best taste of the meal.

Christ tells us that we are to be salt in this world. That means we are to enhance the lives of those around us by getting mixed up in their daily living. If our children are taught to isolate themselves from the world, how can they be salt or light? First Timothy 4:12 clearly instructs us to "Let no man despise thy youth; but be thou an example of the believers, in word, in conversation, in charity, in spirit, in faith, in purity." Plainly, the teaching is for young people to be an example. Who needs the example? The lost world who lives around them and their peers who claim to know Christ but who show no fruit.

Many times parents who have adopted the theory of isolation gather together and become very condemning of other parents who do not "get it." They believe that they are on a higher spiritual plane than those who allow their children out of the box. But I have yet to meet one parent who can take me to the Word of God and support the isolation theory. Granted there were men in the Bible who believed they were more spiritual because of what they did or did not do. These men were called Pharisees, and over and over we find Christ condemning their actions and words and challenging them to a true relationship with Him. Believe it or not, a child's spiritual maturity and growth is not determined by the list of things that he can or cannot do, and it is not determined by where he attends school or if he dates or not.

Existential Theory

In direct contrast to the isolation theory stands the existential theory. The parents who take this position believe that allowing the child to experience as much as possible with little intervention from them will be the best way to help her make the right choices. They are very sensitive to the young person's emotions and feelings. They are still as frustrated and fearful as the isolation parents but for different reasons. They are afraid their child will rebel at their instructions or push them away because of their intervention in her life. This makes following their God-given instincts as parents nearly impossible, which leads to frustration.

The existential parents will make these statements:

"I don't want to do anything to make her upset or mad. This could only turn her away. I just let her know that I am here for her if she needs me."

"She doesn't like it when I pry into her business, so I just hope she is with the right crowd."

"Boys will be boys. They are going to sow a few wild oats, you know kids, but he will come around when he sees it's not as fun as it looks."

Problems with the Existential Theory

When I talk with parents who operate by the existential theory, I find that they fall into one of two categories. Either their children are in constant trouble and they are hoping to ride it out, or they never have any real trouble with their children—not because their children aren't getting into trouble, but because they are completely ignorant of what their children are doing.

In my years as a dean of women, I met many parents in the course of dealing with students' discipline issues. One girl sticks out in my mind as I think of the existential parenting style. She was a girl I was having a great deal of difficulty with at school, because she totally disregarded any rule that she did not feel was legitimate. I finally had to call her parents to discuss the situation. It didn't take long to figure out where the trouble was coming from.

Her parents began by telling me what a good girl she was. She was talented, everyone liked her, she was always attracting the boys, she loved to teach children's church and sing in the choir, and according to them, she was a saint. They informed me that she didn't like rules she didn't understand, so if she didn't understand a rule at home, she didn't have to obey it. She didn't understand why she needed a curfew, so they didn't give her one. She didn't understand why she needed to tell them where she was going and what she was doing, so they allowed her to leave with her friends without any explanation. But they assured me that she had always picked good Christian friends and they had never had any trouble out of her at all. I guess not! I am sure she did not feel they had any right to know all the times she had gone out drinking and clubbing. I bet she did not feel it was important to tell them how many boys she had made out with in the back of the car.

Proverbs 29:15 quickly puts a wrench in the existential theory. "The rod and reproof give wisdom: but a child left to himself brin-geth his mother to shame." Notice it lists "reproof" along with "the rod." Many parents feel when their child has passed the age of spankings that their hands are tied. Not according to the Bible.

Don't leave your young person to himself to figure out what life is all about. Don't buy into the lie that says your child will love you more and respond better if you let him do his own thing. The Bible reminds us that our children will not die when we correct them (Proverbs 23:13). Their feelings may get hurt and they may be unhappy with your decision, but they will not be scarred for life. But when your daughter loses her purity, or lies fighting for her life in the ICU after riding with a drunk driver, those are scars that she has to deal with for the rest of her life. We must teach and train them to be soldiers for Christ because they have an enemy who is seeking to devour them. And the devil doesn't care how he does it, just as long as he gets to them early before they have a chance to make a difference for the Lord.

So if neither building a box to put them in nor giving them enough rope to hang themselves is a good option, then what *is* the best way? God has not left us without a direction map for living. His Word shows us clearly the way that will work the best to ready His little ones for great service.

God's Way: Preparation

Joseph spent years moving from pit to prison before he ever sat down in the palace. Moses spent forty years in the desert before the Exodus. David spent more time in caves after he was anointed to be the next king than he did in the palace. Jesus himself spent forty days in the wilderness at the beginning of his earthly ministry.

God always prepares His people before He sends them out to serve Him. Children are no exception. They don't need to be locked away from the world to be a follower of Christ. They don't need to experience all the bad stuff so they can get it out of their systems and then follow Christ. They need their parents to teach them what it means to follow Christ. Christ will provide the experiences and wilderness moments in their lives to complete their preparation.

As a mother you must concentrate on preparing your children for what the world has to offer. The problems your children face are not that different than those faced by Adam and Eve in the Garden of Eden. Yes, times have changed and the means of temptation have changed, but the core issues have been the same since the beginning of time. Satan is still a roaring lion seeking whom he may devour. He is using every available tool to distract and attack the young people of this generation, just as he has so many generations before. His weapons may be different, but his desire to harm is still the same. So how can you train your soldiers?

Ephesians 6 is one of the best training passages in Scripture. In this passage we are taught how to dress for success in battle. I'm sure you have taught your kids how to get dressed for school, but do they know how to get dressed for battle each day? Teaching your children to put on the armor of God is an important part of raising battle-ready kids. In the military a soldier is issued his gear and then taught what each piece is for and precisely how to use it. Every day his gear and his dress are inspected. I would encourage you to do the same. Teach your children about each piece of the armor and then teach them how to use it.

Once your children trust Christ, their head is covered by the *helmet of salvation*, but their heart can still be exposed. The *breastplate of righteousness* is the piece designed to protect their vital organs. Righteousness is simply doing what is right. Although we live in a world that teaches us truth is relative, we live by God's Word, which gives us a moral code to live by. We need to teach our children that success in battle comes from knowing what is right and wrong and then living according to what is right. This is the key to protecting their hearts and lives as they are in the world each day. We'll look at this in more depth in the next chapter.

The *shield of faith* is another vital piece of the armor of God. Your children must know that they serve a God who can be trusted. In everything God is faithful and is working for their good. If they don't believe this then they will always struggle in battle. I believe the key to holding the shield of faith high is a personal walk with God. For years I had heard that God could be trusted, but as my faith began to be tested, I went from hearing to believing. Job understood this principle when he said, "I have heard of thee by the hearing of the ear: but now mine eye seeth thee" (Job 42:5). As we walk in a real, authentic relationship with Christ our faith grows. Help your children cultivate a walk with God that is real and personal. Then they can lift their shield high knowing that God can be trusted in all areas of their life.

A good mother will plan on victory but be ready for defeat as well. Sometimes our children will fall, but they do not have to fail. When they make mistakes, be there to encourage and console them. Your life must show them the path to forgiveness and grace. Encouraging someone is pouring courage into them so they can get up and try again.

You can encourage your children by praying for them and by teaching them to watch and pray. Although not often listed as a piece of the armor, Paul stresses prayer as a vital part of spiritual warfare. "With all prayer and petition pray at all times in the Spirit, and with this in view, be on the alert with all perseverance and petition for all the saints" (Ephesians 6:18 NASB).

These tools will give you a good place to start as you help your warrior through the transitions of life. Although we wish they never had to fight and we could always protect them, most of us understand that is not reality. Therefore a battle-ready mother must focus on giving them "roots to grow and wings to fly."

Prepare Your Soldier!

A mother's natural instinct is to protect her child from any harm. It is difficult for a mother to protect her twenty-one-year-old as a soldier much less her twelve-year-old. But there is no way to protect him without preparing him. Preparation is the greatest protection we can give our children, because we know that if they are prepared they will be ready to face the challenges ahead of them, with or without our assistance.

I am so grateful for the many parents who have children fighting for my freedom today. It can't be easy to know that your child is in harm's way, and yet I know they are proud of their young people. In the spiritual realm a war rages around us. So prepare your child for battle, because freedom is at stake and many lives depend on your soldier.

Part Two

My Mama Ain't Playing Games

Chapter 6

You're in My Army Now

Rules and Regulations

In March 1958, Elvis Presley joined the Army. Many female fans wept as the pictures were released of Elvis getting his first military haircut. Even though he was the "King of Rock and Roll," the Army spared no mercy as they outfitted him with his uniform and sent him off to basic training. His fame and fortune didn't matter. Elvis would submit himself to the guidelines that everyone else did, haircut and all.

Life is full of rules and regulations that must be followed. Although some of the guidelines seem ridiculous or unimportant, most are there for our safety and protection. While I think the speed limit on some roads is ridiculous, I wouldn't want to drive on the highway if there were no traffic laws. And I would be scared to death to eat in a restaurant if there were no health standards. None of us likes the idea of rules, and yet we all appreciate the protection of living under them.

In my interactions with mothers, I've observed two faulty approaches to rules and restrictions: (1) unthinking repetition or (2) tossing out the rules.

Don't Be a Copycat

Many parents have family rules based on what they have heard their parents or pastor say, or maybe based on some book or ministry. They have not really put a lot of thought or research into the "why" of what they do. They assume that since someone they respect said it, and that person is quoting Scripture, then the approach must be true and should be how their family does things.

These copycatting parents continue to go through the motions even when they see their children struggling or when it makes no sense to them. When a child begins to question the rule, the reply is almost always the same: "Because I said so" or "Because the Bible says so." And if the child wants to discuss this in any way, the parent immediately becomes defensive and charges him with everything from rebellion to blasphemy.

Our children *need* to know why, and their requests to know why are not unreasonable. So why do we react so strongly? Perhaps we have no clue what the answer is! We know what we do, but we have no idea why we do it. No wonder so many young people walk away from everything they have been taught as soon as they are old enough. They have been given no reason to stay.

Such unthinking copycat behavior has to stop. It is very easy to repeat words and phrases that you have heard before. It is easy to do what has always been done. It's easy to worry more about what someone in the church is going to think than whether your children are taught the truth. It takes time to search God's Word and find out why. It takes time to really wrestle the issue out until you have found the place that God would have for you and your family.

When God speaks with a direct command, He almost always gives us insight as to the "why." Of course there will be times when He is silent and does not give us a clear explanation. In these moments our relationship with God comes into play, and we need to trust that He will only command what is best. When our young people begin to understand this principle, it will help them to be obedient when they are asked to do things that they don't recognize as important. Life is full of situations that require our faithful obedience apart from our clear comprehension. The earlier young people grasp this truth the better off they will be.

Don't Throw Out the Rulebook

The second equally harmful approach to rules is to throw out the rulebook. Many times these permissive parents are reacting to their own childhoods. If you were raised in an environment where everything revolved around a list of do's and don'ts that you did not understand, and your spirituality was judged on this list, then you might have decided that "the list" had to go.

Other parents toss the rulebook because when they were children they encountered false teaching or hypocrisy. If you realized that people were twisting the Bible to make it say whatever they wanted it to say, then you may have decided that you can't really trust those in spiritual leadership, so you walked away from it all. Or if you found that those who were the strictest and most legalistic turned out to be living in major sin at the same time they were hollering at you to cut your hair off your collar or lengthen your skirt, then you probably decided that the whole concept of religion is full of holes and gave up. These circumstances and many more like them are the reasons so many of today's parents refuse to put restrictions on their children. They don't want their children going through what they did.

Throwing out the rulebook sounds like the right answer but it's not. "Two wrongs don't make a right." The people in your past were not right for twisting God's Word, but you are not right for ignoring it.

God never intended for the keeping of the law to become our pathway to heaven. In fact His Word teaches just the opposite. In the book of Romans the apostle Paul is trying to make the Jews understand this very fact. In Romans 3 he is making sure they understand that all have sinned. Even those who were trying to keep the law to go to heaven had broken the law. Since they had broken the law, they were sinners and could not get to heaven on their good deeds. All of us are in need of a Savior.

At the end of verse 20, Paul gives his readers a clear reason for the law. The law was given to show men they are sinners. Salvation is through trusting in the work of Christ on the cross. It's by grace, through faith and not works (Ephesians 2:8). God never intended for people to take His Word out of context and add to the clear commands He has already given. He never intended for people to focus on looking good on the outside but to be filled with all types of wickedness on the inside (Matthew 23:23–28). Rules are not the key to righteousness. Our only chance of righteousness comes from accepting Jesus Christ as our personal Savior. But rules are necessary for our own protection, and obeying them brings blessing, as we will see.

Biblical and Balanced

In Deuteronomy 6, Moses instructed the children of Israel to love God with all their heart, soul, and might. Then he instructed them to teach the ways of God to their children. In fact, Moses told them to talk to their children about it every day and to put it on their doors and on their foreheads. He wanted this important truth to permeate everything they did. He wanted them saturated with understanding so that they would make right choices.

Moses wanted the children to understand why they had to obey these rules, and he wanted their parents to know exactly what to say. Moses told them to tell their children three things: (1) you were once a slave in Egypt and it was hard and miserable; (2) God delivered you from all the suffering; and (3) God did not do all that just to make you His slave; He did it so you could be free and so He could do good things for you because He loves you (Deuteronomy 6:4–25).

I think this simple passage of Scripture teaches us a lot about the concept of rules and how to teach these concepts to our children in a biblical and balanced manner. The people of Israel are a living picture of who we are. We too were once slaves, not to a pharaoh, but to sin. The results of sin—anger, selfishness, unkindness, cheating, lying, despair, to name only a few—make life miserable. But Jesus delivered us from the bondage of sin through His death on the cross, and now because of His loving act, we can enjoy lives filled with love, joy, peace, and all the other fruit of the Spirit. Through the gift of the Spirit, we are able to see God's loving intent in His commands, and we are given the desire to obey His commands out of gratitude and love for Him.

More Than a List of Do's and Don'ts

As a mother you have the tough job of teaching your children about rules, and that means more than developing a list of do's and don'ts. Our children must understand (1) the reason for rules, (2) the blessings of obedience, and (3) the connection between rules and relationship.

These three principles are difficult concepts even for adults to grasp, because we all want our own way. Helping our children understand these principles takes time and patience, starts early in their training, and continues as they grow and mature. So it is well worth our while to spend some time here exploring these principles.

The Reason for Rules: A Long Life

Kids think that parents stay up late at night making up a lot of rules to make their children miserable. In their immaturity they cannot see the necessity of guidelines. They feel the older they become, the fewer restrictions they should have. I often talk to teenagers who feel that because they have arrived at the magical age of sixteen, their parents should throw out all the rules and trust them to always make the right decisions. I wish they could only understand that they will never outgrow the need for rules and guidelines. In fact, the older I become the more aware I am of my need for God's guidance. Young people need to understand that rules have a reason.

God knew that children of all ages would question the need for rules. He knew that even adults would question His commands. In Deuteronomy 6, Moses wants to make sure that all the people understand *why* God gave them commands. He tells them to expect their children to ask why, and Moses makes sure that the parents have the right answer. In verses 1–3 the reasons for God's commands (rules), His statutes (prescribed tasks), and His judgments (act of deciding a case, decision) are explained:

> "Now this is the commandment, the statutes and the judgments which the LORD your God has commanded me to teach you, that you might do them in the land where you are going over to possess it, so that you and your son and your grandson might fear the LORD your God, to

keep all His statutes and His commandments which I command you, all the days of your life, and that your days may be prolonged.

"O Israel, you should listen and be careful to do it, that it may be well with you and that you may multiply greatly, just as the LORD, the God of your fathers, has promised you, in a land flowing with milk and honey." (NASB)

Here, in a nutshell, is God's reason for rules: He wants us to live a long time. He knows that Satan is out to destroy our lives. Satan only has the power that we give him, so as we disobey God's instructions we allow Satan room to devastate. Long life is tied to our obedience to God and to our parents. In Ephesians 6 God repeats this promise of long life to children who are obedient to their parents. Too many people's lives have been cut short because they left the safety of their parents' guidelines.

Several years ago I was reading a newspaper and saw a story that I have never forgotten. A fourteen-year-old boy was out to impress his friends at school, so he bragged that he could drive his father's Suburban. His friends laughed at him and challenged him to prove it. The young man hatched a plan that would prove to his friends that he could drive the SUV. His plan was simple: he would sneak out of his house after his parents had gone to bed and drive to all his friends' houses and pick them up for a joy ride. He bragged that they would be back in bed before anyone knew what had happened. The list of those wanting to go on this excursion began to grow, and by the time evening rolled around, eleven middle school students were planning to sneak out.

At around 3:00 a.m. the boy grabbed his mother's keys from her purse and crept out the front door. He started up the SUV and slowly backed out of the driveway with his lights off. Within fifteen or twenty minutes he had picked up six of his friends and was growing confident. As they sped down a curvy back road to pick up the next girl on the list, the young man lost control of the SUV. The car swerved across the road, flipped several times, and crashed head on into a large oak tree. A neighbor who had just gotten home from his job heard the squeal of the tires and the impact of the wreck. He called emergency personnel. When the police arrived on the scene they found the oak tree had split and fallen on top of the car. All seven children were dead.

Reading this story broke my heart. I am sure that each of those children knew they were breaking their parents' rules when they crept from their beds, dressed, and snuck out of their homes. So why did they do it? The kids who were on the list to be picked up but never got in the car were asked the same question. The answer was simple: they didn't think it was a big deal. But their disregard for rules came at a very high cost—their very lives.

The Blessings of Obedience: Protection and a Good Life

Disobedience *is* a big deal. I am grateful disobedience does not always cost so much, but our children need to understand how important obedience is to their well-being. In fact, the primary reason for guidelines is safety. Even small children need to be taught this important principle.

I would like to give you a visual aid that I have used many times as I have talked to young people about this principle. Maybe it will help you as you try to help your children understand why God has given us guidelines for our lives.

Picture James Bond's umbrella: bullet proof, impenetrable, and large enough to cover Bond. If Bond is attacked, the umbrella becomes a weapon fending off evil from every direction. The umbrella serves as his defense from everything that would try to take his life.

What if James got a little cocky and said, "I don't need this umbrella; I can handle things myself." What if he went out every day on his missions without the umbrella? We all know Bond wouldn't last long, because he has enemies everywhere. He might get lucky for a few days and dodge a few bullets, but after awhile something would get him.

God has put an umbrella of protection over His children as well. He protects us night and day from things that would harm us in any way. Throughout Scripture we are told that He is our rock, our shield, our defender, and our strong tower. Nothing comes into our lives that does not pass through the gate of God's protection. God also gives us other sources of protection. Those in authority over us also form a barrier of security around us. Children need to understand that God has provided parents as a source of protection for them as well. Submitting to God and to the authorities God has placed over us keeps us under the umbrella of God's shelter.

God wants to care for us and to be our defender, but He allows us to choose how we live our lives. Obedience to Him guarantees that we will always be guarded and guided by Him. Sometimes I disobey His commands and neglect to listen to His voice. Sometimes I choose my way over His. When I do this I step out from under the protection that God has offered to me. Just like James Bond, I will not make it long without injury, pain, and possibly even death if I continue to leave my source of protection behind. God allows us to make choices with our lives but we cannot choose our consequences. Every decision we make has consequences.

Obeying rules is not only good for our protection. Obedience to God's rules also gives us a good life, one where "it may be well with you" (Deuteronomy 6:3). Obedience to God is not doom and gloom, or even boring, miserable days. Instead, God wants us to live holy (whole!), abundant lives. In John 10:10, Jesus reminds the disciples: "The thief comes only to steal and kill and destroy; I came that [you] may have life, and have it abundantly." Jesus came to give His disciples an overflowing life filled with good things. Even though they would face hard days ahead, He wanted them to know that they could find it all joy in Him.

All of our days are not filled with sunshine either; even our children face difficulties and hard situations. God's plan for their lives is still abundance. His desire for their days is joy, and He promises that they can have these things in the midst of trials and tough times. The key to this type of living is obedience.

Our children must know that sin enslaves us and is a cruel taskmaster. They must understand that God delivered us from the bondage of sin. They must know that God loves them and only desires to do good for them. He wants to free them, not confine them. His commands and instructions are not chains of slavery but are liberties in Christ. When we follow them, we are safe from sin's bondage and its consequences. We are never freer than when we are obedient to God.

The Connection Between Rules and Relationship

Rules will never explain relationship, but a relationship will always help us understand rules. Because God loves us and wants to do good things for us, He protects us. It's that simple. When I realize that my good is His motivation, then my response should be to love Him more. The more I realize He loves me, the more I love Him, and the more I love Him, the more I want to obey Him.

Relationship is built on love—this principle is crucial in the relationship you are building with Christ *and* with your children. The unconditional love of God is our example. God knew all our faults and failures and yet He chose to love us anyway. This love gives us a security and acceptance that strengthens us. When we know we are loved and cared for it is amazing how we respond.

I can remember getting into trouble when I was a kid. My parents would sit down across from me and begin to talk about what I had done. As they talked about how disappointed they were and how they thought they could count on me to make better choices, I crumbled inside. There were times I wished they would have just spanked me because it would have hurt less.

As I became a teenager, I can remember being faced with decisions of right and wrong. As I stood at that crossroad of decision I could always see my parents' faces and I didn't want to break their hearts. Thankfully, the relationship I had built with them kept me from making many poor choices. At those moments I wasn't making a decision because of a rule but because of the love I had for my parents and the love I knew they had for me.

Listen to that again: *I wasn't making a decision because of a rule, but because of the love I had for my parents and the love I knew they had for me.*

Your children need to know that you love them, and you need to *show* that love in both word and action. It's easy to say the words, but words are empty if they are not backed by actions. Relationships take work and time to build. It takes wisdom to be able to love a child in such a Christlike manner that even in his moments of disobedience he knows he is loved. A wise mother will realize that she demonstrates her love as she sets boundaries, enforces boundaries, and shows grace and mercy.

Our heavenly Father has given us His example to follow. As I enter a relationship with God, I stand in awe of who He is and everything He does. This "awe" or "fear," as Deuteronomy states it, also affects my obedience. He is God, so He knows what is best for me. When He speaks I would be wise to listen and obey, because He has my best interest at heart. To disobey would mean leaving the freedom and safety of His protection. Disobedience can only lead to destruction or judgment. The devil will destroy me if I will let him. God will pursue me if I disobey, and He will punish me so I will return to His protection.

Our children must have a relationship with God before they are going to fully understand the blessings of obedience. Hopefully their relationship with God helps them build the right relationship with you as their mom, and they will come to understand that you and God are a team, and you are on their side. You are not out to get them or make their world miserable; you love them and desire the best for them: a long, blessed, and good life.

The Ten Commandments

When I begin to understand how God's guidelines were born out of His love for me, and His desire to keep me on the right track, the connection between rules and relationship clicks. Now I can begin to build my life and the life of my children on solid ground. I start doing this by establishing the non-negotiables.

So just what are the non-negotiables? What are the foundational rules for good living that God has given us, rules that we should teach to our children? Our heavenly Father summarized them in ten, easy-to-remember commands. Let's take a brief look at them here.

1. *Worship God alone.*

Teach your children that the God of the Bible is the one, true God, and He revealed Himself in three persons: Father, Son, and Holy Spirit. This truth is the bedrock of everything they will base their lives on. Their eternal destiny is based on this truth, and so is their quality of daily living on this earth. Jesus said in John 14:6, "I am the way, the truth, and the life: no man cometh unto the Father, but by me." This precept is not popular in our culture, but popularity has no bearing on truth.

2. *Do not make idols for yourself.*

When you think of idols, do you think of little wooden statues or some Greek god or goddess? If so, you probably feel you can skip this section and find another commandment that better fits your household. But before you rush on, remember that an idol is anything we put before God. You might not have statues in your home, but are there things that take priority over God and your relationship with Him? Who or what sits on the throne of your life? If we are not careful we can allow a hobby, a person, or a job to become more important than God.

Young people have the same struggles. Many of them are dedicated completely to a sport, a game, a boyfriend, or a group of friends. Their lives revolve around the things they place in the spots of top priority. God should not just be *one* of those top priorities; He should be *the* top priority. If He is not, then we have an idol in our lives. God makes it clear in Exodus 20 that those who worship idols will suffer for generations to come, but those who put God first will be blessed by His love and His kindness.

3. *Do not misuse God's name.*

What are ways that we misuse the name of God? Sure, we could curse His name or use His name for a curse word and that would be blaspheming the name of God. But there are many other ways that we can misuse His name and thus take His name in vain. One way we can do this is by using His name flippantly and without thought. Jesus cautioned against vain repetition in prayer. Have you ever caught yourself repeating the Lord's name over and over in prayer without any purpose or meaning? Have you ever sworn to keep a promise and used His name to seal that promise and then failed to do what you swore to do? Do your slang terms refer to God in some way? In all of these ways we misuse God's name. His name is holy and not one to be taken lightly. Listen to your children's words and teach them the importance of honoring God's name in their conversations.

4. *Observe a day of rest and worship.*

If you have noticed, every one of the commands we have discussed has touched upon our relationship with God in some manner. The command to observe the Sabbath is no different. God gave His people a day dedicated to resting and enjoying His goodness. Although this command in its strictest sense is not required for believers today, the principle of this command is expected by God. In fact, taking time out to rest was instituted long before the days of Moses. God Himself "rested" after six days of work as an example of what we should do in our own lives. Sabbath is an important time for families to spend the day together resting, eating, and celebrating God's provision. It is also a way to demonstrate their trust in God to provide for them on the day they do not work.

Have you become so busy that you have forgotten God's principle of Sabbath? For many of us Sunday is the day when we go to church, worship the Lord, and spend time with our families. But I know so many people who are involved in their church ministry to such a degree that Sunday is one of their hardest days of work. If that describes you, then you need to find another day when your family can gather, rest, and worship God for His goodness. Your children need to understand this important principle or they will begin to believe that the world cannot get along without them. This discipline should be initiated early in the life of a child, and then stay consistent as they grow busier.

5. *Honor your father and mother.*

At this command the emphasis turns from our relationship to God to our relationship with others. The first earthly relationship God emphasizes is the relationship between parent and child. So much is encapsulated in the word *honor*: obedience, courtesy, and respect, just to name a few. I am sure you have quoted this commandment to your child on many occasions and maybe you have gone so far as to make her memorize it, but does she understand what it means?

Honor is more than just doing the right thing. I have watched many children obey their parents as they mumble under their breath, slam things around, and look as if they are going to explode. If you allow your child to get away with that, he will miss the big picture. Honor requires his attitude, actions, and words to be right as well. It is this combination that God promises to bless with a long and full life.

6. Do not kill.

God is the giver of life and therefore, He is the only One who has the right to take life. God knows the number of our days and has a purpose for each of them. God has written this law so strongly on the heart of man that even those who do not accept the truth of God's Word recognize it is wrong to take another person's life.

The Bible does allow for people to kill when they are involved in a lawful war, in self-defense, and as a punishment for a crime. These concepts are important for our children to understand because we live in a time of war and violence. In addition, they need to understand that hatred is akin to murder (Matthew 5:22).

Your children need to be taught the sanctity of life. As you teach this precept, find opportunities to discuss abortion, euthanasia, and other important cultural issues in light of God's Word. Then your children will have more than a commandment—they will have a biblical worldview.

7. Do not commit adultery.

Things that defile the body are just as important as things that destroy it. These acts of defilement are what the seventh command-ment addresses. In this age, marriage is being attacked on every hand. The world's philosophy is very relaxed when it comes to the marriage vows because they do not understand the importance of covenant relationship. If we are not careful, our children can be influenced by Hollywood's ideas when it comes to marriage. Many times cheating is represented as expected, humorous, and good for a healthy relationship. Make sure your children understand how God hates this sin. In Hebrews 13:4, God makes it clear that "Marriage is to be held in honor among all, and the marriage bed is to be undefiled; for fornicators and adulterers God will judge" (NASB).

8. *Do not steal.*

Although you may have never robbed a bank or stolen someone's wallet, all of us have been guilty of taking something that was not ours sometime in our lives. Maybe it was fifty cents on your brother's desk, a pack of gum from the convenience store, or an answer from the girl's test who sat next to you. All of those are stealing.

Through the years of working with teenagers, I have been blown away at their propensity to steal. For many stealing is a game; they want to see how much they can get away with. In talking with them, I found that they do not see their crime as serious or important. Today's young people steal songs, games, clothes, food, and other people's work. Teach your children that when they steal from others they are violating God's law and cheating themselves in the long run.

9. *Do not bear false witness.*

What does it mean to "bear false witness" against a person? Simply put, it means that we should not speak or testify falsely against another person. This would include lying about someone, deceiving someone, or wrongfully accusing someone of something they did not do. It is difficult for us to face the truth when we know there are negative consequences. It is much easier to lie about it or blame someone else. One of the greatest character traits we can help build in our children is the value of being honest and taking responsibility for their own actions.

10. *Do not covet.*

It's interesting that God ends with this command. When you think about it, many of the other commandments that deal with our relationship to our neighbor are tied to this one. We covet when we long to possess something that is not ours. In the previous commands

God has instructed us to not take a life, or another person's possessions, or another person's spouse because they do not belong to us. It all boils down to our own issues of discontent and greed.

Who's on First?

Our children are surrounded by a culture that teaches "it's all about you." They need to learn to see with the eyes of God and to love with the heart of God. To do this, they must put away the old man with his lust and jealousies and put on the new man.

Many years ago the comedy team of Abbott and Costello had a famous skit about baseball called "Who's on First." Around and around they would go with the question, "Who's on first?" until the audience finally realized that the person on first base was named "Who."

Here's the question I would like to ask you: "Who's on first?" When it comes to establishing the non-negotiables in our lives, it all comes down to who has first place in our life. If God is first, as the first four commandments instruct Him to be, then obedience to Him will be our highest priority.

When asked to name the greatest commandment, Jesus summed it up in one simple statement: love the Lord with all your heart, soul, and mind, and love your neighbor as you love yourself. You see, when God is in first place in our lives, then we have the ability to love others.

Ken Collier, a friend of mine, made this statement in a service I attended over twenty years ago, but I have never forgotten it. "Only two choices on the shelf: loving God or loving self." I pray that we can teach our children what it means to truly love God and love others.

Family Guidelines

Once you have built the right foundation with the Ten Commandments, you can begin to lay out the guidelines for your home. These guidelines will be a combination of principles and precepts from God's Word and additional guidelines that you as their parents feel would be best for your family. Make sure your children realize the difference. Bible rules should never be broken, and there are no circumstances that make it okay to disobey God's commands. Family guidelines, however, are not the same.

When I was growing up, we had Bible rules and Bowman rules. Bowman rules were policies that my parents had set forth for our home. Although many of them were tied to biblical principles, not all of them had Scriptural significance. For instance, one Bowman rule was no television or playing until the homework was finished. My dad didn't have a chapter and verse for this one, but I knew it was our family's policy.

When I went off to college, my dad wasn't there to enforce this family policy. There were many times that I would have been in big trouble if that Bowman rule was still my responsibility to obey. It would have been good for me to have still followed this guideline because there were many times, especially in my freshman year, that I should have put homework first. But I was not disobedient to my dad because I goofed off first. As I matured, I wisely learned that Dad was pretty smart when he came up with that policy and I reaped the benefits of that practice.

There will be many instances in our children's lives when they will have the opportunity to make their own choices. You need to make sure they have a clear grasp of when they can choose and what they can choose.

As you decide what rules are best for your family and as you attempt to explain your family rules to your children, think through the "whys" of your policies and pair your guidelines with solid reasons. If you can't find a reason for your policies in Scripture or in practicality, maybe you should throw them out. Don't just do it because that is what everyone expects. But remember, don't throw it out just because you hate the arrogance of the "list keepers."

The Three P's

One of the simplest ways I have found to teach young people about discerning right from wrong is "The Three P's." The Bible teaches us rules for living through different methods: precepts, principles, and preferences.

Precepts are when the Bible clearly teaches that a particular behavior is a sin. For instance, "Thou shalt not kill." The Bible is clear that murder is wrong.

Principles are when the Bible teaches a right from wrong by application. The Sermon on the Mount is a great illustration. In Matthew 5, Jesus reminds the people of the Ten Commandments (the precepts). But then He goes on to take the precept and expand it into daily application.

> "Ye have heard that it was said by them of old time, Thou shalt not kill; and whosoever shall kill shall be in danger of judgment. But I say unto you, That whosoever is angry with his brother without a cause shall be in danger of judgment." (Matthew 5:21–22)

Jesus is trying to teach the people that being obedient to God and being blessed by Him takes more than just obeying the letter of the law. Anger begins in a person's heart long before a murder takes place. So the principle is simple: Don't sin in your anger, and you will never have to worry about murder. God uses principles to guide our every day lives throughout His Word. It is important that young people learn to recognize the principles as well as the precepts.

The Bible also leaves some things up to our preference. These are areas where it would not be a sin to go one way or another. I once heard someone say, "Where the Bible is silent, I dare not be dogmatic." What a great truth. If the Bible is not clear on a certain area, then it is important that we give others the grace to choose differently than we choose. Many of our young people are confused because for years they have been taught that a particular behavior was wrong according to Scripture. Then they actually begin to study Scriptures themselves only to find out that it doesn't teach that at all. We hurt ourselves as leaders and guides of young people when we are dogmatic in teaching things as truth that are not.

You must determine what the Bible teaches and how. When the Bible teaches by precept or principle, then we have no choice in our actions. In order to be obedient to God, we must follow His direction. Teach your children how much God loves them and how His only desire is for their best. He would never tell us "no" to hurt us or to ruin our lives.

When it comes to preferences, make sure that your children know that God's Word is not dogmatic in every area and that good people choose differently. You can still let them know how your family is going to choose on these issues, but when they encounter another Christian who has made a different choice, it's okay. When young people grasp these simple teaching methods, they respond much better to the guidelines they are given.

If we build our children's foundation on truth, when they grow older and begin to make their own decisions, they will make them based on truth. In certain areas they may not make the same choices that we would like for them to make, but if they base their guidelines on biblical truth, they will do just fine.

Chapter 7

A Few Good Men

Building Character

༺༻

For years the military has relied on slogans to advertise and inspire young men and women to join their ranks. I am sure you remember some of these:

- Be All You Can Be (Army)
- The Few, the Proud, the Marines
- We're Looking for a Few Good Men (Marines)
- Aim High (Air Force)
- It's Not Just a Job. It's an Adventure! (Navy)

If you look closely you realize that although each branch was saying it differently, they were all saying the same thing. Each branch was trying to demonstrate that if you joined them you would elevate yourself above the crowd.

In 2005, Alex and Brett Harris, younger brothers of author Joshua Harris (*I Kissed Dating Goodbye*) founded *TheRebelution.com*. At the time Alex and Brett were only sixteen years old. These young men decided that they were tired of living the status quo life. The official definition of the "rebelution" is "a teenage rebellion against the low expectations of an ungodly culture." Alex and Brett put it this way:

When you look around today, in terms of godly character and practical competence, our culture does not expect much of us young people. We are not only expected to do very little that is wise or good, but we're expected to do the opposite. Our media-saturated youth culture is constantly reinforcing lower and lower standards and expectations…. The "rebelution" has really become a type of counter-cultural youth movement among Christian young people … [who are] returning to biblical and historical levels of character and competence.[5]

These guys are on the right track. We need children to get excited about taking it to the next level and to call their friends to action. It's a revolution that is needed in our day and time.

I am convinced that mothers can be part of this call to action. It will require a counter-cultural mindset and an aggressive approach, but it's possible. By focusing on key aspects of character building, we can shape a few good men — *and* women — who will honor Christ with their lives.

Self-Concept

Today we hear a lot about building a child's self-esteem. Books and articles abound on ways to help children feel good about who they are. Unfortunately, many of these ideas are empty and will not make a difference on a consistent basis. Yes, children need to have the courage to step out and do challenging tasks or believe they have what it takes to do the hard thing, but strong self-esteem will not develop from repeating mantras or deflating the grading scales.

I have worked with young people from a variety of different angles: coach, professor, counselor, and friend. Each one of these angles has taught me something different about self-image and how it's built. In practicality I have learned more from my role as a coach regarding self-concept than any other role. Here are some tips I have learned through the years from coaching that I have seen help young people take positive strides.

Treat your child with respect and expect him to treat you the same way. Humiliation is never a good technique. When you demean a child on a regular basis, he will end up hating you. It saddens me when I hear parents tell their child he is stupid. Children remember the names they are called, and many adults still bear the scars from those names. If you need to deal with your child, find a private place to do it and choose words that build, not destroy.

Avoid comparing your child to a sibling or to another child. Each child is different, even those who come from the same gene pool. Children have their own strengths and weaknesses. When a young person feels that she has to be like someone else, defeat immediately sets in. They know it's impossible for them to be like the other child. What they assume is that you like one child better than the other, and it hurts when you are on the low end of the deal. It's easy for parents to wish that their middle child would eat her vegetables like their oldest. It's okay to encourage Sally to eat her vegetables like Billy, but as a parent you cannot make statements like "Why can't you just be like Billy and eat your vegetables." I know people who spent their whole childhood in the shadow of another sibling and it still affects them today as adults. Obviously you as a parent see the differences in your children. Make sure you keep a balanced view.

Don't be a "performance-driven" parent. I can't tell you how many times I have talked to an athlete who was terrified of playing because her parents were coming to the game. When asked what the big deal was, these athletes always told me that they never seem to be able to play good enough for their parents. One girl put it this way, "If I have a good game my dad is all smiles and hugs, and if I have a bad one, he starts lecturing me about what I should have done the minute he sees me."

The pressure children put on themselves is already great enough without parents adding to the pressure in areas of performance. Your love and acceptance should never be conditional. Your children should know that if they did their best you are proud of them. And if they really mess up and blow it, they need to know that you love them despite your disappointment in their choices. Too many times parents are more concerned with what others are thinking about their children. At this point, the focus becomes embarrassment, and the child's needs have taken a backseat to the parent's needs. Children are going to embarrass their parents. It's a statement of fact. So quit worrying about what other people think of you or your children. Give your children the freedom to be themselves and do their best, even if they are not the best. Allow your child to walk to the beat of his own drum as long as the walk is biblical. And when he disappoints you and makes a poor decision, consider his feelings and his struggles more than your own pride.

Threats will never move you forward. I have found that threats are not the best for moving a child from one spot to another. Whether in discipline or in motivation, a threat only removes the positive pressure of responsibility in choice. Let me explain. When you threaten a child in discipline ("Billy, if you do that one more time I will …") and you don't follow through, that child immediately knows you don't mean what you say. They have just learned that they can push you further, which is the opposite of what you are trying to do as a parent. When you threaten in a motivational setting ("Billy, if you don't clean your room no one is watching television tonight") you are attaching a negative to something that you want to be a positive. This always means the negative wins. Oh, Billy might clean his room, but he will probably do the job half-heartedly. He will probably grumble and gripe the whole time and never have the right attitude.

As a parent your goal is to stretch your child and push him to reach his potential. In order to do that you must *challenge* him. Challenging is much better than threatening because it's positive in nature. Backing up a challenge with encouragement and praise lets your child know that you believe in him and think he can do it. Challenges usually end with a sense of accomplishment, even if the complete goal was not met. When possible always tag a challenge with a planned outcome. For instance, "Billy, I know that your room is a mess and that you think you will never get it clean. But here is what I know about you: you can clean this room and you can do a great job in less than thirty minutes. I have a challenge for you; I will set the timer for thirty minutes and then I will come and inspect your room. When you make it, and you will, we will all have a special treat in honor of your great accomplishment. I know you can do it."

You can't imagine the results I have seen through the years by changing my tactics from threats to challenges. Of course in certain areas of life children have responsibility to do the basics without any fanfare. Challenges are for areas where they need a push, not for areas where they are being disobedient. If you have set a rule in place that homework must be done before the television can be turned on and one of your children disobeys, then this is not a time for a challenge but for discipline.

Praise in public, criticize in private. Nothing can humiliate a child more than being embarrassed in front of others. There is a time and a place for correction and discipline. Even small children are affected by this and should be considered. If possible, remove your child from the public situation in a calm and quiet manner. Move to another room in your home, even if just the family is around. You will be amazed at the difference in your children's response to you when you remove their need to be defensive and protect themselves. This works especially well when dealing with boys, because it takes the bruised ego out of play. But even girls do better because it enables them to keep their emotions in check.

As a basketball coach, I read anything that Dean Smith wrote. He coached the North Carolina Tarheels for almost forty years, and is one of the winningest coaches in college basketball. He once said that when a player really blew it on the court, he would wait two or three times up and down the court before he substituted him out. Then he would have the player sit down right beside him on the bench, and he would sit there and look straight ahead watching the game while simultaneously letting this player have it for his mistakes. No one in the stands knew what was going on, and that player was never embarrassed.[6]

Coach Smith knew how important it was to keep his players' confidence high. You may not have a whistle or run a practice, but as a mother you do coach a team. So keep your children's confidence high by whispering the criticism and shouting the praise. Praise has high value. When your child does something well, make sure you praise her. If your teen is struggling, look for things to praise her for. Don't force it or praise her for something that is not legitimate, but when you see progress, even at small levels, heap on the praise.

Failing is a part of life; failure is not. Everyone makes mistakes. Learning anything new usually requires a series of failed attempts before beginning to catch on. There is no area of life that is an exception to this rule. Whether it be sports, academics, music, or even a new job, mistakes are part of the process. Parents must be reminded that children will not be good at everything. They will not make A's in every subject. It is important that we have a realistic picture of what our children can accomplish and then encourage them to work hard and do a little bit better. Parents can do so much harm to a child's confidence when they expect more from her than is possible.

It's okay to be average in certain areas of your life. It does not mean you are a failure. In fact, we are all average in many areas of our lives and below average in some. But God has gifted all of us with certain talents and abilities where we excel. These are the areas He wants us to use for His honor and glory.

Children need guidance in this area of their lives. They need someone encouraging them to try and not to be afraid of failing. They need to understand that God has given them great talents. As a mom, you need to help them find these talents. It may not be in the area of sports or something common. Cheer them on and help them learn that a failure is a person who quits altogether and refuses to keep trying just because he makes mistakes.

Important Character Traits

What is character? It's not something you are born with or that naturally drips from your pores. Character is something that is developed along the way. Paul teaches in Romans that tribulation and trials come into our lives, and these hard circumstances build perseverance and patience. This maturing process builds character in our lives (Romans 5:3–5). Andy Stanley in his book *Louder than Words* defines character as "the will to do what is right, as defined by God, regardless of personal cost."[7]

Children are often called characters, but I wonder how many of them *have* character? If you understand that character is something that is developed in a person over his or her lifetime, then you as a mother have an opportunity to make a difference. If our young people are going to impact their world they cannot follow the crowd. The crowd is in chaos, always looking for something new and something exciting. Character development is anything but exciting from the perspective of the crowd. The crowd is going to encourage your child to do what feels good. Character is going to require him to do what is right, regardless of how he feels. When character appears, the crowd disappears. Andy was right: doing what is right will cost.

Honesty

There are many attributes that would describe good character, but let's start with honesty. Teaching your children to tell the truth is one of the most valuable things that you can do for them. Today we live in a world where the truth is flexible. Truth can be bent to fit your circumstances or your situation. Society has become so accustomed to lying that we really don't think much about it. Deception has become the norm. Children need to understand that being honest is important. There is no situation that can justify a lie.

Integrity

Integrity is closely tied to telling the truth because it is your willingness to stand by what you have promised or stated. People of integrity stand by their word and their principles. Young people need to see this trait modeled. Adults, especially those in leadership, need to guard their words so they can consistently follow through on what they say. Children will grasp the exceptions more easily when they have seen consistency modeled. They need to understand that their reputation is being built based on their ability to stand by their principles.

Responsibility

Children need to learn that they must accept responsibility for their actions before they can assign responsibility to someone else. Many parents today refuse to let their children take responsibility for their actions. They sweep in and come to the child's aid by blaming everyone else but the child. This is one of the worst things you can do for your children. Owning my actions gives me the control to deal with my mistakes and move past them. When it's always someone else's fault, I have no control.

I am not saying that you should never defend your children if they are in the right, but you should teach them that life is full of unfair moments. One of the greatest acts of humility and one that takes great courage is the ability to say, "I am sorry, will you forgive me?" It is hard to do, but as your children learn to face the truth and admit to their wrongdoing they will find the freedom that can only come from forgiveness. This will impact their emotional health and will teach them much about their relationship with God.

There are several areas that can help teach responsibility at home. One way that is very effective is to teach your children about money and finances. Since this is an area they will deal with all of their lives, it can only help to begin early. An allowance is a great place to start. Start out with a small amount of money each week and a designated place to put that money. Teach your children to save and to spend their money responsibly. Requiring them to pay for their activities or toys is a good way to begin teaching them the importance of spending their money wisely.

Another important principle of money is tithing and giving. Each time they get money they should learn to take ten percent and give it back to their local church. They should also learn to help those in need. Giving to help worthwhile charities or other people who have great need is a good way for children to begin to learn the difference between wants and needs.

Respect

Another important character trait that must be built at home is respect. I am often amazed at the lack of respect our children demonstrate. Yet I know that respect is a character trait that is taught first and expected second. As I talk to kids about this issue many of them don't seem to realize that their definition of respect is incorrect. Some young people think you have to agree with someone to respect them. We don't respect ideas but people. You can show someone respect and still disagree with them. If our children don't understand this concept they will struggle in holding down a job, in obeying the law, or even in sharing the gospel with others. Demonstrating respect to others regardless of their beliefs, race, or creed is necessary if we are to be followers of Christ.

Jesus met many people during His earthly ministry and without exception treated them all fairly. One example that stands out to me is the woman at the well. She was a Samaritan, a people the Jews despised, and yet He was not concerned with her heritage. An adulterous woman, she had many husbands and was currently living with a man she was not married to, and yet He was not repulsed by her sinfulness. Jesus saw beyond all the issues to the only thing that mattered: her soul. He showed her great respect and love.

Children learn respect from how we as adults treat them and how we treat others. For many parents the idea of showing their children respect is a foreign one. But if we want our children to show respect to us, we must also show them that same respect.

Manners

What ever happened to manners? When I was growing up I always understood manners were directly linked to respect. I was taught to say "Yes, sir" and "No, sir" because it showed respect to my elders. My brothers were taught to hold the door for girls and for those who were older because it showed respect. I guess it would make sense that if respect were in jeopardy then manners would also be on the decline.

I recently heard someone say that teaching your children manners was pointless because who could determine what was correct and incorrect. I thought about this for a long time trying to find the reasoning behind it. It's true that people designed the rules of etiquette and politeness. And it's true that no one died and left Emily Post as the manners police. So who came up with the idea behind manners and etiquette, and why should we follow their lead?

Actually, the Bible gives us some of the core values behind what we now call manners. In Matthew 7:12 Jesus gave us the Golden Rule and instructed us to treat others the same way we would want to be treated. All of us desire to be treated with respect and dignity. We show people respect by treating them kindly and showing them a servant's attitude. In John 13, Jesus taught His disciples the principle of a servant's heart by washing their feet. In fact, He even washed Judas's feet, knowing that he would leave that very night and betray Him.

Forty years ago a child who did not demonstrate good manners stood out like a sore thumb. Today a child who exhibits good manners stands out. Although it is not necessary to know every rule of etiquette for every situation, your children will benefit greatly from basic table manners, respect to elders, and appropriateness.

Appropriateness

Your children need to know that certain environments call for certain types of behavior. At home it is okay to be rough and tumble and crazy. A church is not the place for such behavior. At the ballgame it is okay to wear old faded jeans and a sloppy t-shirt, but at a wedding it is not appropriate. As your children learn that being appropriate shows respect to those around them, they can start to apply these basic principles to other areas of their lives.

Recently I was eating in a restaurant. At the table across the aisle from me sat a young man in his early twenties who wore a pair of faded, torn jeans. His shirt had a stain and looked as if it came from the bottom of a pile of laundry. His hair, hanging down over his face, needed a good combing. Had he been sitting there eating I probably wouldn't have noticed his dress at all, but he was not eating. He was filling out a job application.

I watched as one of the managers came over to the table dressed in a shirt and tie. Although the restaurant was not upscale by any means it was still a nice place to eat. Each person who waited tables was dressed nicely. I listened as the manager quickly ran down a list of questions regarding his experience. The interview was brief. Don't call us, we'll call you, and the young man was gone.

As I got up to leave the restaurant I noticed the manager interviewing another young man who was about the same age. He had on an ironed pair of khaki pants and a polo shirt. His hair was clean and neatly combed. He sat up straight as he talked to the manager. As I paid my bill I saw the two of them get up. The manager shook his hand and led him up to the checkout area, where another employee met him with a company shirt and apron. "Thank you, sir," is all the young man said as he took the clothes for his new job and left.

Two young men needed a job. They both went to the right place to get that job, but only one left with it. Knowing what is appropriate and when is an important skill for life. It will give your children the leadership skills they need to stand out in the right way. It will open doors for them that are closed for others, and it will give them a good reputation wherever they go.

The book of Ecclesiastes teaches us there is a time and a place for everything. Our children need to understand that certain discussions are not appropriate in mixed company. They need to be taught there is a time to dress casual, but there is also a time to show respect by dressing nice. We have clearly missed the mark with this generation because today's young people do not understand this concept. Society teaches them to dress like they want when they want. But that is not a realistic way to live. Many adults have jobs where a dress code is required. I know of some businesses that are so picky they tell their employees what colors to wear. We are doing our children a great disservice if we do not prepare them for the real world they live in.

Teamwork

One of the most important concepts for a person to grasp if they are going to build godly character is teamwork. We live in a world where it's all about me and my needs and my desires. The culture is teaching our young people to fight for their rights and demand to be heard. The idea of teamwork—striving together for a common goal—is becoming a thing of the past. Too many young people are being taught by the example of professional athletes and movie stars that life should revolve around them.

Every team member has a role to play, and your house is no different. Give your children roles and responsibilities. Make sure they know that each person in your family is counting on them to do their part. When they step up and do more, make sure you acknowledge their effort. You might be surprised at what your children can accomplish at home, at school, and in their community. Help them dream big dreams and encourage them to take the next step. If they know they have the entire family team behind them they can accomplish amazing feats.

I am a perfect example of this team concept. When I felt the Lord calling me to step out from my job at the university and begin to speak and write, my family was the first to know. Immediately they stepped up and began to ask how they could pray and how they could help. Over the next few years many people told me I was crazy and advised me to go back to the great career I had left. My family never wavered. Their support continued to be the comfort

I fell back on when it seemed I had lost my mind. I would not be where I am today without their backing.

Several years ago I felt that God was leading the ministry to host our first conference. It was a large undertaking and a huge step of faith. I pitched the idea to my family and they thought it was a great idea. One by one they came to me asking how they could help. One of my greatest concerns was how I was going to keep everything going and focus on the messages I would deliver that weekend. Teamwork saved the day. My brothers volunteered to work on the stage. My sister-in-laws volunteered to organize the many people who help run the event. My mother handled the registration process, and my dad was our runner. My assistant Lisa took care of the program, and every member of the board at Dare for More Ministries took a task and ran with it. I was amazed at how smoothly the event ran. God blessed us with so many women that first year, and I still get emails and letters from dear women whom God touched at that meeting. It would have never happened if it had not been for selfless individuals who became part of a team.

I have learned that God-sized goals are usually larger than one person. Teach your children the value of being part of a team. Encourage them to be a part of at least one team along the way. Sports are a great avenue, but there are also drama teams, debate teams, Boy and Girl Scouts, 4-H, and many other opportunities for young people to begin to learn the value of teamwork.

Respect for Authority

Your children must learn to respect authority if they are going to get very far in life. God has placed authority over us in many different forms, and we don't always get to pick and choose our leaders. Not all authority will be followers of Christ; many of them may be wicked and ungodly, but that should never keep us from submitting to them and showing them respect.

In Romans 13, Paul reminds Christians who have to submit to wicked and ungodly rulers that God is the one who establishes authority. As long as the authority does not ask me to do something contrary to Scripture, then I am to obey. When I disobey authority, I am disobeying God. Children need to be taught that they don't always have to *agree* in order to *obey*. They will meet many people along the way who they will disagree with, but if that person is in a position of authority, they need to obey.

Attitude

Submission to another person is a difficult thing. It is hard for any of us to keep our mouths closed and show respect to a person who is asking us to do something we don't want to do. This is why it is vital to teach children the proper way to ask questions and to approach adults in authority. As they learn at home with their parents, hopefully they will carry this out the back door and into other arenas. Teachers, employers, coaches, and those who work with young people take quick notice of a child who shows respect through having the right attitude. Submission will always get you further than the wrong attitude. Attitude is so vital.

Years ago when I was just a student in high school, I tore the ACL in my knee and was recovering from surgery. I was angry and frustrated at my situation. This injury would keep me from playing basketball that season and maybe the next. I was struggling with my attitude and my focus. Then I read these words in a book by Chuck Swindoll, a passage that is so famous that I've seen it quoted frequently in the years since then:

> I believe the single most significant decision I can make on a day-to-day basis is my choice of attitude. It is more important than my past, my education, my bankroll, my successes or failures, fame or pain, what other people think of me or say about my circumstances, my position, or me. Attitude is that 'single string' that keeps me going or cripples my progress. It alone fuels my fire or assaults my hope. When my attitudes are right, there's no barrier too high, no valley too deep, no dream too extreme, no challenge too great for me.[8]

God used this single statement to remind me of what was important and what He could do through me if I only had the right spirit. To this day I have never forgotten that statement or the importance it has played in my life.

If you will take the time to teach your children about the importance of submitting to authority and having the right attitude, it will pay big dividends in their lives as they grow older. As a parent you will reap the benefits of children who can follow directions because they were disciplined enough to listen and give you their undivided attention. You will enjoy working with your children because you will have developed a loyalty to each other that is stronger than your disagreements.

Commitment to Excellence

"If you are going to do something, do it right the first time." I don't know who penned these immortal words, but up until a few years ago I thought it was my mother. My mother has never been a lollygagger. (A lollygagger is a North Carolina term for someone who takes way too long to do something because they are goofing off.) The dust never settled under her feet. She would wear me out just watching her. There was always something that needed to be done, and she was always doing it.

Mom tried her best to instill that virtue of excellence into her three children. My two brothers and I were taught how to clean a house from top to bottom and how to do it right. Being the oldest, I was assigned the tougher jobs. My brothers got to empty the trash, pick up the clutter, and put the toys away. I had to scrub the bathrooms. It was horrible.

Early on I reached a conclusion, the faster I worked, the sooner I was done. So I quit wasting time trying to talk Mom out of it and quickly grabbed the necessary equipment and headed off to my task. At first, I would clean a bathroom in less than five minutes. I soon realized that this was not going to cut it with Mom. As I stood before her declaring that I had cleaned the bathroom in less time than it took her to carry her load of laundry downstairs, she would scowl at me and march me back to the bathroom. After showing me the obvious lack of cleanliness, she would leave me to try again.

It took only a few times of this for me to realize I had to wait longer to go and get her. So I would do my usual quick-clean routine and then waste the appropriate amount of time. Surely now she would believe that I had done a good job. Mom was wise beyond her years and caught on to this ruse quickly. In utter disbelief she would march me right back to that bathroom repeating those famous words, "If you are going to do a job, do it right the first time."

I know there were many times it would have been much easier for her to have just done the job herself and sent me off to play. I am sure that she thought I would never get it, but I did. I still hate housework, but because of Mom's faithfulness to push me and teach me, I know that a job worth doing is worth doing right … the first time!

A person who does her best at everything stands out in a crowd. When I was coaching I used to give a coach's award every year to the player on my team who best demonstrated this trait. It's not a common trait or one that always makes the headlines, but it makes the biggest difference in the lives of everyone who is touched by it. A person who takes pride in what she does and determines to do the best she can with every task assigned to her will go a long way.

Most people will work hard while you are watching, but the minute you turn your back they slack off. Others will work hard at jobs they enjoy or things that get them applause but will half-heartedly do anything they dislike. Excellence takes a commitment. It requires sustained effort over a period of time. People with this kind of integrity will do a good job at whatever you assign them.

Excellence is biblical. Colossians 3:23 gives us the key to excellence: "And whatsoever ye do, do it heartily as to the Lord and not unto men." Many children will memorize this verse, but how many of them understand the importance of practicing it? Regardless of who is watching or how much you are being paid, do it right. Children need to learn they are not living to impress people; they are living to glorify God. God is glorified when we do our very best for Him regardless of the task. Teach your children the value of excellence and help them to commit to doing everything they do to glorify God.

Values Matter

Parents begin to instill a code of values into their children at an early age. It may not be intentional or well thought out, but the values are passed along nevertheless. Children incorporate these values from what adults say and what they do. Toddlers learn they cannot touch certain objects and if they do, they will get their hands popped. This teaches them that certain objects are valuable and important and must be left alone. Six-year-olds learn that they cannot take food into the pretty room with the white carpet. This teaches them that certain rooms have a higher value than others and must be protected. Ten-year-olds learn that when Dad is reading the paper he cannot be disturbed. This shows them how to respect their father's need for rest. The list can go on and on. We speak volumes without saying a word. Our actions identify our values and the levels of those values. As children grow and begin to mentally process their surroundings, they come to understand this value system, and it becomes a part of their lives as well.

When I was growing up we lived in a home with a large front yard. My dad always kept that yard looking sharp. The bushes were always hedged and the grass was always a beautiful rich green color. I had spent hours as a toddler sitting on my father's knee as "we" mowed the yard together. As I got older I wanted to learn to mow the yard myself. So my dad began to teach me.

My dad would always take the first few rounds around the yard to make sure I had a path to follow. He would match the mower up just right so that the current blade path just barely overlapped the last one. Then he would stand and watch as I climbed on the mower and began to mow. I would glance back at him to see if he thought I was doing a good job, and he would smile and point for me to pay attention to where I was going. Finally he would walk away to crank the push mower and do the trim work.

For the next few minutes it was my yard and I was determined to do a good job. Of course as a typical kid, I would soon get distracted. I would be watching the dog or waving to the neighbors, paying no attention to the path I was supposed to be mowing. The flash of my father's long strides across the yard would snap me back into reality. His piercing whistle hit my ears like an alarm, and I knew something was wrong. I quickly turned in the direction he was pointing and waving and realized that I had swerved off the path and had left a huge strip of grass uncut.

I can't tell you how many times that happened as I was growing up. Sometimes my dad would make me climb off and he would fix it, mow a few rounds, and then let me climb back on. Other times he would patiently stand and holler out instructions as I tried to fix it myself. He put up with a lot through the years teaching three children to mow, but he taught us the value of a job done well.

My father instilled many more values in my life besides the ones I learned mowing yards, and those values have stayed with me through my lifetime. What values are your children learning from being a part of your family? What do your lifestyle choices say about you? What about your schedule? Do your day-to-day activities and priorities reflect the values you want to teach your kids?

Now, more than ever, values matter. Character matters. Now, more than ever, we need to "aim high" and make sure we raise more than "a few good men" and women. It will take consistency, repetition, and patience. You have to believe in them more than they believe in themselves.

I will never forget my first college basketball team. I had a young team and I knew that if they were ever going to be successful they were going to have to learn a whole new way of playing. Every day I would introduce a new concept in practice and we would drill until they got it. But the key to their success depended on their ability to make the right choice in a game situation and for everyone else on the team to respond appropriately to that choice.

I can tell you that there were times when I felt that practice had been a waste of time and no one was listening. There were times when the opposing team seemed to know what we were doing before we did, but we kept working. I refused to give up. The girls would get discouraged and want to go back and play the way that came naturally to them, but I wouldn't let them. It took almost two years, but I will never forget the day it all came together. We were playing a team that had beaten us in the past by more than twenty points. With twenty minutes to go in the game we were down by twelve. With the ball in our hands we began to make our passes. Suddenly one of my girls recognized what was happening and responded correctly; we scored. Next time down the floor it happened again; we scored. The girls on the bench hit their feet and began to cheer. The girls on the floor smiled and began to gain confidence. They made it look easy as time after time they came down the floor and scored.

The other team was confused and called a timeout. I didn't say much in that huddle because I didn't have to. My captains looked at me and said, "Coach, we can do this." And they did. That night we won by sixteen points. The coach for the other team asked me what happened to my team. I just smiled and said, "They finally got it."

Mom, don't give up. Character, values, integrity, and excellence do not come easily. And there will be no greater moment than when you see them get it. That moment when all your hard work and effort has paid off, and your children make you proud to be their mother.

Chapter 8

Live Fire

Are They Ready?

Soldiers must be trained in live-fire situations if they are going to survive in the heat of battle. Live fire is a rehearsal for the real thing. It's a test to see if they are ready and if they know how to use the equipment and training they have been given to defeat the enemy. One of the great benefits of live fire is the soldier has a chance to fire his gun without worrying about an actual enemy returning fire.

If you are going to be a battle-ready mom who raises battle-ready kids, then you must create a home environment that will give your children "live-fire" experience. This gradual elevation of risk will help them be ready to stand boldly and face the enemy knowing they are protected and prepared.

As with all training, there are "crawl, walk, and run" steps that must be taken. No one understands that concept more than a mother. I am sure you remember watching those little ones scoot across the floor in their first attempt to crawl. Before long they were grabbing the coffee table and taking their first steps along the side. It's so amazing how resilient they are. They just keep falling and getting back up to try walking again. Soon they are on the move and you can't keep up with them. That is the process; you have to crawl before you can run.

The same is true with life training. It starts when children are young and continues until they are grown. Along the way you will watch them fall and struggle to get back up again. A mother's natural instinct is to run and grab them and help them up, but an experienced mother learns that allowing them to fall, struggle, and succeed on their own is an important part of their growth. No mother wants her son or daughter to fall in an area that will destroy their lives. That is why it is necessary to start early in their development.

Get in the Know

I am always surprised to find out how much parents don't know about the trends of the day. Even though their children are constantly talking about the latest craze and are begging for the latest technology, parents seem to be oblivious to exactly what their children are talking about.

One December I met a woman at Walmart who was looking for a video game for her son. He was ten and he was going to just die if he didn't get it for Christmas. Because the store was so busy and I knew where the games were kept, I offered to show her. I soon found the game and discovered it was rated V for violent and M for mature audience. As I read the description of the game I realized it was nothing more than a killing spree via computer. There were weapons of every sort, people got their heads cut off, and body parts were lying around on the ground—all in the name of fun.

I knew I was probably overstepping my bounds, but I just had to say something. I started gently although inside I was reeling. "Ma'am, did you say your boy was ten?"

She nodded. "Yes, he just turned ten last month."

"Did you know that this game is rated violent and mature?"

"What does that mean?" she responded wearily.

She had asked the wrong person. By this time I was fired up because people are so foolish to make games where killing people is a sport. I read the description to her. I explained to her the warning labels. After all that, I was stunned to see her take the video game and place it in her cart. I looked at her in utter disbelief.

She must have read the look on my face. "He will be so disappointed if he doesn't get it," she said defensively. "All his friends have it, and he plays it over at their houses all the time. I guess it can't be that bad if their mothers let them have it. You know how it is; they just have to put those labels on there so you can't sue them." With that she turned her cart around and walked away.

I still get steamed up about it all these years later. I wondered as I wrote these words where that young man is today and how things turned out for him. I wonder if his mother ever realized that her ignorance and apathy were dangerous.

Parents have to know, and that means you have to work at learning information that is not interesting to you but that is interesting to your child. It means you have to take the time to find out, firsthand, what is going on in his world. Don't take the word of other parents that something is acceptable or unacceptable. Take the time to find out for yourself. Only then will you be able to explain your position to your children. They may not always agree with you, but they will respect the fact that you took the time to find out and that you know your stuff.

Many mothers don't understand the importance of the facts. Their philosophy is "We don't let our kids do that, so why do I need to know anything about it?" Kids know. The older they get the more they know what you do and do not understand about their world. I encourage parents to be the first to bring up relevant subjects with their children. Talking about popular celebrities, movies, books, or even the latest hits on the radio brings you into their world. Culture being what it is, your children are knowledgeable about these subjects even if you have family policies against them. When they realize that you know a good deal about these areas, they will be more open with you about their questions and about what they know.

So how do you get in the know? I will share with you the things that I do to stay up to date on the latest fads and trends. I am sure you can think of more ways, but these have always seemed to work for me.

Magazines

One of the best sources of information is still the magazine. There are many magazines dedicated just to teens, such as *Cosmo Girl*, *Girl's Life*, and *Seventeen*. There are others that are dedicated to current trends and pop culture, like *People*, *US*, and *Star*. You can browse while you stand in line at the grocery store or as you sit with a coffee at your local bookstore, or you can check them out free from the teen section in the library. Look at the articles, note which celebrity is on the cover, and browse through the advertising. This will give you a good start to knowing who and what is "in."

Google and the Internet

Make a list of topics, slang words, or people that you want to learn more about. Then Google them—type in the key words you are looking for in the search window. The Internet is also helpful when you hear your children use terms you do not understand. Most of the time you can type in that word and perform a search to get the definition.

While website popularity changes daily, you will want to view whatever site comes up in conversation. Maybe it's a video clip on YouTube, or an online game. Some websites that are currently popular with teens include teenchat.com, cartoonnetwork.com, and real.com. Of course the social networking sites such as Facebook and MySpace are always big hits with young people as well.

There are also websites that exist to help inform parents. Focus on the Family's pluggedin.com provides details on movies, television shows and more. I would encourage you to go and check out the site, and then bookmark it so you can come back to it often for information on current teen issues.

The Youth Pastor, Coach, or Schoolteacher

Some of my best "informants" are those who work with young people every day. They hear more than parents do, and they tend to be up to date on the latest verbiage and issues. So don't be afraid to ask them questions on certain areas you are trying to learn about.

Important Issues to Discuss

Mothers frequently ask me what age they should talk to their children about sex. This seems to be the main issue on the average mother's mind as her children mature. Although this is a legitimate question and one I will address in depth later in this book, I am concerned that so many other important issues are not coming to a mother's mind.

Did you know:

- 17.9 percent of eighth graders, 41.2 percent of tenth graders and 55.1 percent of twelfth graders have been drunk at least once?[9]
- 15.9 percent of eighth graders, 21.9 percent of tenth graders, and 25.9 percent of twelfth graders report having consumed alcohol during the past month?[10]
- 3.3 million (13 percent) of children between the ages of twelve and seventeen receive services for emotional or behavioral problems in a mental health setting each year?[11]
- 16.6 percent of youths between the ages of twelve and seventeen used cigarettes during the past year and 12.9 percent used marijuana?[12]
- 90 percent of eight- to sixteen-years-olds have viewed porn online?[13]

There is so much to talk about with your children. If they live in this world, they are being exposed to temptations from every angle. At some point you will need to address the issues of drug use, alcohol, smoking, pornography, violence, cursing, and so on.

Emotional issues are also important to discuss with your children. Turmoil in the home, divorce, trouble at school, being bullied, a breakup with a boyfriend, or even not getting enough time to rest can cause high levels of stress in young people. It is vital that parents stay informed about these issues so they can quickly spot problems. Children need to know they are not alone. They need to be taught how to deal with hard situations. Their schedules need to be guarded so they are getting plenty of rest.

Don't assume that your children will never face these issues; assume they will. Spend time talking to them about all the areas that could destroy their lives. Listen to them and allow them to dialogue with you about these issues. Keep pointing them back to truth as you equip them to take a stand for what is right.

Know Your Weapons Well: Prayer, Scripture, and Worship

As you prepare your children for live-fire situations, make sure they are well armed with a Christian's primary weapons: prayer, Scripture, and worship. Just as you teach your children to be physically healthy by showing them the importance of good food, rest, exercise, and hygiene, you can also teach your children the basics of spiritual health, and the daily habits that help to build a strong faith.

Prayer should be an important part of the atmosphere in your home. Although a prayer before you eat is important, your children should know that mealtime is not the only time to talk to God. Pray for tests, projects, ballgames, and recitals. Pray for their requests and things that are important to them, but also make sure they make time to pray for others. One of the important benefits of prayer is that it helps us to get our minds off of ourselves and on others. Teach your children to value prayer and make it a part of their daily lives.

When you are young it's hard to comprehend the value of God's Word. You can't imagine how much you need God's Word and how powerful it is. If we are not careful, children get the idea that reading the Bible is just something they have to do and they don't see the value of it. Show your children that the Bible is our guidebook for life and the only way we will know which way to go. When your children are younger they will rely on your example and your study time to guide them. As they get older they should begin to value the importance of their own relationship with God and begin to seek their personal time in the Word. Help your children see that God's Word is truth and let them see you using it over and over in practical ways to help steer your family's decisions.

Church is an important part of the life of every believer. Attending a vibrant, exciting church that teaches and preaches the Word of God is part of God's formula for a healthy believer. Many children grow up in church, but when they reach their teen years they decide they no longer like it. Sometimes it's just a phase they are going through, and other times this indicates a real problem. If you have a child who is struggling with church attendance, prayerfully ask God to show you the root of the problem. In so many cases, children have never been taught why God designed the church or why it is important for a believer to attend. All they know is that they always have to go. So help your children understand the value of church. Make sure you are attending a church that is growing and that provides something for your children at every age. If you don't enjoy going, it's really hard to fool your children, so make sure your church is a place *you* are excited about being a member. Sometimes you may feel your teen needs a break. In that case, give them a breather from youth activities but not from church attendance.

Teach Truth *and* Critical Thinking Skills

What do your children really believe? As we found in the last chapter, our children need to know God's rules for living, and they need to be taught right from wrong. They also need to understand that there are absolutes in this life that they can stand on. They need to be taught that truth exists, and it sets the standard for all our choices. Life is not a series of random situations with relative options. The Word of God is truth. Belief matters.

The Bible teaches important truths that our children must understand, believe, and be able to defend. Christians living in today's world need to be thinkers. They need to know *what* they believe and *why* they know it is truth. This is the only way they will be able to share their faith in a world that is hostile to the gospel. When they enter the world they will be faced with live-fire situations every day. People will test their beliefs and their convictions. As they grow older it will become more popular to debate the truth and doubt the proven. You must build their foundation strong and prepare them to answer the questions that are hurled at them.

Show your children what it looks like to listen to someone you disagree with and show them respect. Teach them how to communicate their beliefs in a way that makes sense. Point out deceptions and lies that can easily infiltrate a person's philosophy of life and affect his ability to see truth clearly. Talk to them about faith and what it means to believe in something that you cannot see or touch. Help them to see the evidences of their faith so they realize their faith is not blind. Christianity is not a wild leap of faith; there is much evidence for its validity.

If you feel you need help learning to defend your faith, there are many great resources that will help strengthen you. Lee Strobel, Josh McDowell, and Ravi Zacharias have some great tools to help. All three of these men have websites, books, and sessions to assist you in learning to defend your faith. Your children need to know that their beliefs are founded on a bedrock of truth, not fairytales. They need to be confident in their understanding of God and His Word.

A Biblical Worldview

One of the greatest advantages to live fire is that it is a test that has clear results. Live fire allows the instructor to quickly know which soldiers are getting it and which are not. In the military, instructors use these exercises as teaching tools. Once the drill has been conducted they will walk back through the drill and show each soldier his good and bad decisions. Then they teach him how to do it better next time.

Making sure your children assimilate a biblical worldview can also be taught and tested with clear results. Every day is filled with teachable moments. These are moments that clearly illustrate something you want your children to understand. Use these teachable moments as present-day parables to teach your children a biblical worldview. Topics such as honesty, lying, and cheating fill our daily news reports. Television shows and movies are filled with opportunities to hit the pause button and check your children's worldview. It may amaze you what they actually believe.

A woman came to me in uncontrollable tears one afternoon after I had given a session for mothers. Her daughter had a friend who had gotten pregnant outside of marriage. It was a small town so it was the topic of conversation everywhere she went. Her daughter was upset that everyone was talking about her friend and in her disgust told her mother that she had recommended her friend get an abortion so she wouldn't have to go through all of this. The mother sat stunned at her daughter's admission.

I asked the woman how she responded to her daughter. She sat across from me weeping and wringing her hands. "That's the real problem," she said, "I didn't know what to tell her. I didn't know what to say. I know abortion is wrong, but I couldn't take her to one verse and prove it to her." After she had talked to her pastor, researched the subject, and armed herself with the truth of God's Word, she sat down again with her daughter and discussed the whole issue.

It's easy to say you believe something until you are called on to prove it. We are pragmatists by nature; we do what is convenient and what works for us, and we can bend any truth to make it fit our case. Our children need to know that God's way is best and unbending. Lying is wrong, even when it's just a "white lie." Cheating is wrong, even when you studied and just can't remember the answer. Pornography is wrong, even though you are not physically with the person. And the list goes on. If children are going to survive in the heat of the battle, they must have truth to fall back on. They must know what the Bible teaches and how it pertains to their worldview, and they must make the application from head to heart on a daily basis so that it's fleshed out in their lives.

As they grow older, you will see their beliefs demonstrated in their words and actions. Use these teachable moments to show them their strengths and weaknesses. Help them develop the ability to look at life through the lens of God's Word. Only as they learn to see life God's way will they find true freedom and success.

Dealing with Temptation

Dealing with temptation is not a matter of "if" but of "when." The devil will stop at nothing to ruin our children's lives. His goal is to find their weakness and go at it hard. Parents usually know their children well enough to identify their weaknesses. You can help your children recognize the areas they struggle in and arm themselves for victory.

I think we have done our children a great injustice because in many church circles we talk a lot about sin and about temptation, but how many times have you heard someone preach a sermon on fighting temptation? It's easy to get the idea that we don't actually expect to defeat Satan. We expect to lose. We expect to sin. Then we go to God, after months of guilt and confusion, and ask His forgiveness only to return to that same sin in a few days or weeks. We have bought the lie that this is just the way it goes. We live in defeat and rarely experience the victory that God promised to us.

The apostle Paul did not buy into this lie for one second and neither should you. In First Corinthians 10:13 he reminds us of a very important promise:

> There hath no temptation taken you but such as is common to man: but God is faithful, who will not suffer you to be tempted above that ye are able; but will with the temptation also make a way to escape, that ye may be able to bear it.

God knows that we will face temptation, but He is faithful and will not allow Satan to tempt you beyond the limit of His power in our lives. God will make an exit door, or as the King James Version puts it, "a way of escape."

When I fly I try to get a seat on the exit row for more legroom. The flight attendant will then stop by to ask two questions: can you open this door if you need to, and can you help others out? Everyone else on the plane is only told one thing about the exit rows: in case of an emergency, find the nearest one, and get out! Sitting in an exit row brings responsibility. I am so glad that Jesus Christ sits in our exit row. He can open the door, and He can lead us out. All I have to do is find the door, and He will lead me out.

Teaching children to find the exit door is part of your job as their mother. If your child is the type who is easily swayed, teach him to say no or to stand up for the truth. If he is the first to head off into trouble, remind him of the serious consequences of disobedience. Teach your children to literally walk away from dangerous or questionable situations and people. Or use the story of Joseph and Potiphar's wife to teach them that at times they just might need to *run* (Genesis 39:12)!

Remind your children of these other truths we learn from Scripture about dealing with temptation as well.

First, God does not ever tempt man to do evil. Satan is the only one who tempts us to do evil (James 1:13). Satan tempted Jesus on many occasions, but He never sinned (Hebrews 4:15). When Satan tempted Him in the wilderness, Jesus gave us a great demonstration of how to deal with temptation, using Scripture to counterattack. Hebrews 2:18 reminds us that because Jesus was tempted, He can help us pull through.

Temptation literally pulls us away from God and what is right and pulls us toward evil. James 1:14 tells us that we are tempted when we are drawn away by our own lust and enticed. Even though we trust Christ and He gives us a new nature, we still have to say no to sin because we still have that old nature too. But what has changed is our ability to have victory through Christ. The Holy Spirit now lives in us and empowers us to do the right thing.

The devil is our enemy and he hates us, but we are not left to make it on our own. Jesus gave us protection so that when we are shot at we won't be wounded. Ephesians 6:11 commands us to put on the armor of God so we can stand against the devil. There is a piece for each area of temptation. It would be a good practice to verbally put these pieces on every day as you pray and ask God to help you.

James 4:7 promises us that if we will resist the devil he will leave us. He does not have a choice. We *do* have a choice though. God doesn't want us to sin, but we still can choose to do wrong. If we are going to do what is right we have to be ready to run for the exit door when temptation comes. First Corinthians 6:18, 10:14; 1 Timothy 6:11; and 2 Timothy 2:22 instruct us to flee from sin and the temptation to sin.

One day it will all be over. Revelation 20:10 victoriously proclaims that in the end Satan loses.

In order to prepare your children for the attacks that will come, you must arm them with these truths. The devil is not playing games, and we can't afford to sit back and hope our kids make the right decisions, especially if we have not prepared them.

Perfect Practice Makes Perfect

Vince Lombardi was one of football's greatest coaches. He is often noted for his pithy sayings. "Practice does not make perfect. Only perfect practice makes perfect" is one of them. As a former coach I understand the point he was stressing. You have to do it the *right* way over and over again if you are going to get it right the majority of the time.

The home is our children's greatest practice field. This is the place where they should be able to work on getting it right. The time to try and fail is during the years when they are surrounded by their parents, pastors, and many other adults who care for them. Granted we don't want to see them fail, but we know that they have to learn, and failing is just as much a part of learning as success.

Parents must be there to help their children work through the hard times and the bad choices. As our children grow in Christ and are discipled, they will begin to make good choices. They learn and they grow in their relationship with God, and their hearts begin to *want* to do what is right. The Holy Spirit empowers them to make wise choices and to say no to temptation. And God puts His hand on them and on the gifts that He has given them and uses them to do great things for Him.

Mothers are great cheerleaders for their children. They see potential when no one else does. But if your children are going to reach their God-given potential you must prepare them. They must hear your voice first and loudest. They must be prepared to defend what they believe and stand for what is right, not because they have been told but because they understand the teachings of God's Word and have thought it through. And they must have the opportunity to practice these skills in a safe environment before they leave your home as young adults.

Chapter 9

Mommy Sonar

Do You Recognize the Signals?

Can you hear your child's cry? When you first brought her home from the hospital you probably listened to her every move. Those first few weeks, it seemed you couldn't relax. If she was sleeping you were worried she wasn't breathing or something was wrong, and so you were up and down checking on her. If you bought a monitor and put it in the room and all was peaceful, you were sure the monitor was broken, so you got up to check on it. Now several children down the road, you can't even hear your six-year-old screaming "Mom" for the one hundredth time, at the top of her lungs, standing only five feet away.

Time and experience have taught mothers that things usually turn out all right and most of the time "emergencies" can wait. But deep within the heart of a mother lies the God-given instinct to be protective of her children and to be concerned for their well-being. This instinct causes a mother to know when something is going on before anything has been said. This gut feeling keeps mothers honed in to the signals their children are sending.

During the early stages of World War II, our Navy began to train submariners to work with sonar equipment. This new technology was very important to the submarines because it allowed them to see and hear what was around them without surfacing to periscope depth. Sonar works by making use of an echo. Sound waves are sent into the environment by an object or an animal, and some of them bounce back. Sonar equipment can send out a sound that will ping off any object around it, thus allowing the person listening to identify how big the object is, how far away it is, and even what it is.

Each sonar operator has to be able to distinguish the different sounds that are detected in the water. Sonar can pick up sounds made by submarines, torpedoes, or sea animals. It could mean the difference between life and death for a whole crew if an enemy submarine was mistaken for a whale or missed entirely because the crewman didn't listen intently. The sonar systems became so effective that submariners had to be very quiet to avoid being detected by other submarines. The crew would wear tennis shoes to silence their footsteps!

Sending Out Signals Every Day

I believe in "Mommy Sonar"! We need mothers who are intent on listening to their children's heartbeat. In many cases it can make the difference between survival and sorrow. Your children are sending out signals every day. They want to be noticed and heard, even though they always seem to have their tennis shoes on. Despite our preconceived ideas, they want to be given direction and guidance by their parents. How are your listening skills?

Do you know your child? Do you watch your child the way you used to in those early weeks? Have you become so busy with your own life and schedule that you sometimes forget you have children?

Josh McDowell reported that the average parent spends less than ten minutes in meaningful conversation with their children on a monthly basis.[14] Can you imagine what shape our country would be in if our Navy submariners only listened to the sonar equipment ten minutes a day? Many of our children are suffering great injury at the hand of the devil because parents are not willing to spend more than ten minutes with them. As a mother you must not only train them, but you must stand guard as their protector while they are learning to stand on their own two feet. One of the best ways you can help them grow strong and be prepared is to learn to hear the difference between a dolphin and a torpedo.

Children communicate in many different ways. As they advance from one age level to the next, their communication styles will change. Many times they will have trouble verbalizing what they are feeling to you so they will find other means of communicating. These attempts will not always be positive, but parents must make the effort to understand what their child is trying to convey. Communication is so much more than just discussions. Watching their facial expressions, their posture, their attitudes, and their tone will help you determine what is going on in their lives. As you mesh these signals with what you already know about your child's personality and temperament, you will begin to identify his communication style. Once you have accomplished this, you are on your way to knowing the difference between a dolphin and a torpedo.

What is so amazing about this type of listening is that you have to recognize both the dangers and the natural environment that surround your children. A child's environment dictates much of how she responds. If a child feels safe, she will open up and feel more freedom in sharing. The minute a child detects that she is not being heard she will shut down and tune you out. If there are others around who are listening, it will affect what she says and how she says it.

One of the most powerful illustrations of this effect is the influence of your child's friends. Nothing has the power to change a young person's demeanor and attitude like her peer group. Time and time again I have watched a young person who had a sweet spirit and was really trying to talk to me about a certain problem completely change if her friends walked up and entered the conversation. I learned through the years to anticipate the change and let her off the hook for the moment by changing the topic or just letting her know I would talk with her later. Sensitivity to the environment and the influences affecting your child's behavior is so important to communication. Parents who are willing to make the extra effort to analyze their child's situation will reap the benefits and have a better understanding of their child.

Focused Attention

One of the best ways you can stay on top of things in the life of your child is through focused attention. As a mother your day is filled with distractions. Mothers are multitaskers, moving from one scenario to the next and juggling many responsibilities at once. In the average household this is necessary to keep things running smoothly; however, it is vitally important that you plan time to give each of your children focused attention.

You will never completely understand your child on the outside of his life looking in. So many parents find themselves in just that position because for years they have been too busy. After a while, your child will stop trying to get your attention and will resign himself to talking to others or dealing with life alone. It's not uncommon to hear parents say they don't feel they know their child anymore. The dangers are too great for you to let that happen. You must find the time to focus on your children and their world.

I have found through my years of coaching that passion is a key factor in making a difference. I thoroughly enjoyed coaching players that had passion to go along with their skill. In fact, I would take a player who had less skill and more passion over a player with tons of skill and little passion. The same can be said of mothers who make a difference in the lives of their children. You must have a passion for your children. I am confident that mothers who have a passion for their children, a desire to learn, and a willingness to work at it every day will develop an instinctual ability to read their children.

There are several ways you can incorporate focused attention into your daily routine. Watching several key areas will usually give you a clue when there is a problem and show you where to look for answers.

Behavior

Start by studying your children's behavior. Is the way they are reacting typical? Their typical behavior should be defined by how they act in a comfortable, familiar environment. In most cases, kids are most at ease when they are at home, surrounded by the people they know and love. Anytime you see your child deviate from what you would define as normal, pay close attention. Of course, all of us have good days and bad days, and your children will too. As you learn the difference between a bad day and abnormal behavior, you will begin to become more sensitive to problems they may be facing.

Some key areas you should focus on to establish a normal baseline are a child's facial expressions, tone of voice, and attitude.

Although there are some children who cleverly disguise their emotions behind a stoic face, most young people reveal much about how they feel about things on their face. We all have telltale signs that are quick indicators of our emotional well-being to those who know us well. For children, their eyes, smile, and expression tell a story. Learn to recognize your children's nonverbal indicators. These will help you know the difference between tired and sad, between hurt and mad, and between grumpy and upset. You have to be *especially* aware of your teenager's indicators. Sometimes teens just need a little space, and sometimes space is the *last* thing they need! Knowing your child's indicators will help you determine when and how to approach.

We are all creatures of habit and usually have established patterns that make us more predictable. The trick is the ability to recognize your child's patterns. You must start by learning to filter out the inessential and to bring to the forefront the indispensable. It's easy to jump to conclusions based on quick assessments and begin to rant and rave. Many times the conclusions are wrong and because listening has not taken place, an important door of communication has been closed. As you learn to watch for related behaviors, you will find patterns emerging. These patterns will help you to understand your child and the situation. Don't look at one single trait and jump to immediate conclusions. Be patient and retrain your brain to look for meaningful patterns. As you get better at this skill, you will find that you can quickly assess a situation with great accuracy.

I love to play those computer games where you search for hidden items and piece clues together to solve a puzzle. Working with young people is often much like those games. It's your job to look carefully for the clues that are hidden in plain site. Many times the key is right in front of your nose, but you are in too much of a hurry to notice. Sometimes it's camouflaged well, but if you will slow down, taking in every detail, it will jump out at you. If you detect a signal that doesn't seem quite right, then slow down and begin to look for other signals that might relate. If you begin to find a group of related signals, this is usually an indicator that you are on to something. When you add the signals to the behavior, you then begin to uncover the story.

Working with teens has taught me to be observant of the small details about a person: hair, clothes, body language, and even the way they walk are all indicators of who they are and where they are. When you observe the little details ask yourself, "What are these things telling me?"

Once you know your child's personality and how she responds normally, it will be easy for you to spot when she is "acting." Watch her interaction around friends, classmates, and siblings. This will help you to understand what she is all about.

Some of your children might be more like you, while others are entirely different. Even if you share a similar personality, learn to read your children through the spectrum of their own personality, style, and love language. This is the best way to pick up on inconsistencies in their behavior.

As I have mentioned earlier, tone of voice is one of the most valuable tools in determining meaning. Many times people have been conditioned to say the right things, but the tone in their voice or the inflection used are clues to a hidden thought. Most of the time these thoughts do not match up with the words that come from their mouths. Look for a match. If they ramble when they usually are concise, give short answers when they usually give long drawn-out details, or if they simply don't respond at all, your attention should go to alert status.

Environmental Changes

When a submarine enters enemy territory, everything changes aboard that vessel. Every sailor is on high alert to any change that would send him into action.

A child's environment today is very volatile. School, home, church, and friends all play a role, and any changes in these areas can make a big difference in their lives. Even though you may try to shield your children from difficulties and hardships, they are usually very quick to pick up on any problems. Financial struggles, marital issues, family tension, and a host of other home-related issues can cause changes in them. When home-related issues arise, raise your level of alertness. Look for changes in your children's normal personalities and in their patterns. Dramatic changes usually indicate a powerful struggle. For instance, if your child is normally very neat and tidy and suddenly her room is a complete disaster, you should go on alert. If this change becomes a pattern, then something is wrong. Begin to watch for other signals that something is out of line.

Separation, divorce, moving, changing schools, the death of a loved one, puberty, and sickness are just a few of the major circumstances that can affect children. If your child is experiencing any of these, then you must watch for changes and try to engage her in as much communication as possible. The idea that if you don't talk about it, it will just go away eventually is not really true. You can sweep it under the rug if you like, but that only makes a larger bump in the rug. Help your children to work through major changes by listening to them and providing the security and comfort they need.

Seek First to Understand

In Stephen Covey's book *The Seven Habits of Highly Effective People*, habit number five is this: "Seek first to understand, then to be understood." According to Covey, communication is the most important skill in life, because in order to effectively interact and influence people you must first understand them.[15]

In order to understand we must ask the right questions so the conversation continues and we can learn valuable information that helps us know how to respond. Most of us work in reverse order, meaning we begin to develop opinions and advice before we have completely heard everything a person has to say. It takes concentrated effort to listen intently and attempt to understand what your child is trying to communicate to you.

In addition, take the time to reflect on what they are saying in the light of who they are as a person. When you begin to ask questions, start with assumptions you have already made as you were listening. Ask questions that will either confirm what you were thinking or contradict your ideas. Remember, this is not an interrogation or a job interview—this is your child. Your goal should be to understand them and to clarify what they are thinking. Make your conversation relaxed and as natural as possible, even if the situation is tense. So many times young people shut down because they pick up on our strong emotional reactions and immediately assume they will not be heard or believed.

Every parent should work at incorporating these communication tips as they interact with their children. I know that you will see a difference in the way they respond to you. I also think you will be amazed at the increase in understanding you will have toward any given situation. As you develop this pattern with your children, you will find they will feel more freedom to discuss issues with you. They appreciate a person who does not overreact and begin to judge them before hearing and understanding.

Shortly after September 11, 2001, I had to fly to a meeting. It was the first time I had been in an airport since the upgraded security measures had been put into effect. What a different world it was. The Homeland Security Office displayed warning levels in and around the airport. These levels were color-coded, and the higher the intensity of concern the more security measures were in force. This same principle can be applied as you listen to and observe your child. Distinguishing between the trivial and the urgent will help you know how to respond. In fact, one of the greatest outcomes of this type of listening is your ability to discern between the major and the minor. As you let your understanding guide your level of concern, you should find yourself confident in your instructions and stable in your emotional response.

Lies and Deceit

Despite your best efforts to read your children and understand them, they still have a sinful nature and will be prone to lies and deceit. However, observation skills will allow you to detect when your child is lying. As you begin to decipher your child's natural disposition, the abnormal will stand out to you. You will notice subtle changes in the way they respond. Most people are different when they lie. The differences may be minimal, but if you know your child, you will pick up on them.

I have been lied to on more occasions than I care to remember. Part of my job as the dean of women was handling the disciplinary issues of the female students. I have watched students wiggle and squirm their way from one lie to the next in order to keep from being disciplined. Girls can be great liars. They have a way of turning on this innocent look and charming smile that can be very deceptive. Over the years of working with the girls I began to develop the ability to notice the differences in a truthful person and a liar. A person's posture, gestures, and basic movements can be clear indicators that they are not telling the truth. Learn to look for these changes as you talk with your child. After awhile you will discover their individual indicators that they are not telling the truth. Although these are not 100 percent accurate, they are good gauges of honesty.

It's amazing what focused attention can teach us. I am convinced that if you will take the time to study your children and get to know their hearts, you will become an expert at mommy sonar. And your children will thrive in the knowledge that they are being watched over and cared for.

Chapter 10

Diversity Among the Troops

Your Unique Child

Much of basic training in the military involves giving up individuality. Soldiers dress alike, have similar haircuts, operate on the same schedule, and follow numerous rules and regulations. However, as soldiers rise in the ranks and get to know their own strengths and weaknesses—and get to know each other—their true identities begin to be revealed. One gets promoted, another demoted. They give and get nicknames. They know who to trust and who to avoid.

Most moms I talk with are anxious about having their kids fit in. Like sergeants they hover over their children, making sure their hair is combed, they're dressed properly, and they obey the rules. While some of this training is useful for getting along in society, all the pressure to fit in and look the part can make it easy for individualism to get lost. Kids struggle to find the balance between being their own person and being accepted. Some conform entirely, becoming little robots. Others rebel and become nonconformists, showing a great deal of radical individualism but very little true identity.

Helping your child to find his own style and to be confident with the way God made him is one of your jobs. As a mother, you see your children's unique personalities, gifts, and abilities. This gives you the opportunity to encourage and train them in a way that is especially designed to recognize and appreciate their individuality.

A Diverse Creation

I am so glad that God did not decide to build robots. When God made the world, He created a diverse and wonderful universe. Every snowflake is different. The animal planet is filled with an amazing collection of differences from bugs to whales. Plant life covers the earth with everything from kudzu to giant redwoods. Even "the heavens declare the glory of God and the firmament sheweth his handywork" (Psalm 19:1). God loves variety, and humans are no exception to His pattern of design. We are all very different, but God has a purpose in our assortment. First Corinthians tells us that He made each of us with our own set of personality traits, talents, and gifts so that each of us can have a part in the body of Christ (1 Corinthians 12:14–26). We are all important to God's greater purpose, and we all have a role we must play.

I think mothers may understand this pattern of diversity better than most. Mothers are usually the ones who notice the slightest differences in their children. Mothers are usually able to detect the talents and contributions each child brings to the world. Even though children are bits and pieces of their family tree, they are still unique with their own style.

Since there are no cookie-cutter children, there can be no cookie-cutter parenting. You may wish that you could build a mold of the perfect child and drop your children into it, but good children come in all shapes and sizes. There is a concept in Christianity that all good Christian kids act and look the same. I am afraid that we have confused holiness with personality. In many churches a standard is held up for the "perfect, holy person." In some church circles the emphasis is on how a person dresses, or what version of the Bible they carry. In other circles, it's about how submissive or quiet you are. In his book *Perfect Love*, Jimmy Johnson reflects on this idea. "I'm convinced that 90 percent of the problems in churches … is not 'sin,' but trying to force others to conform to our definition of 'spiritual' temperaments."[16]

If you are going to bring up your children in the "nurture and admonition of the Lord," you need to realize that the Bible does not dictate a certain personality for all good Christian kids (see Ephesians 6:4). Children are as different as snowflakes. Parents must realize their differences and raise them to be the people that God created them to be. God's desire for all of us is that we live holy and sanctified lives. He desires that we submit our personalities, gifts, and abilities to Him so that He can mold us into His image. Only God can transform a person to be more like Him and yet still be just like herself.

A Visionary Mother

Mothers are visionaries for their children. They see what their children can be. They see what it will take to give them a chance to reach that goal. However, seeing their potential and fighting to see that they have a chance to reach it are two different things.

Many of us were glued to the screen during the 2008 Beijing Olympics as Michael Phelps won eight gold medals. He is the most decorated Olympic athlete of all time. It was truly amazing to see him win by a mile and a millisecond, but there was someone else that I enjoyed watching just as much as Michael—his mom! As he swam she jumped, hollered, grimaced, crossed her fingers, and held her breath. In his closest race when no one really knew who won until the announcement was made, she collapsed in her seat almost in utter exhaustion when they finally showed that her son was first.

In an interview published in *ADDITUDE* magazine, Debbie Phelps discussed what it was like to raise a boy who has grown up to achieve such great things. He had problems in school. His teachers complained he couldn't pay attention and was distracting to others. The kids picked on him because he had big ears and long arms. His mom and dad divorced when he was just a little boy. Michael was diagnosed with ADHD at nine years old. This doesn't sound like the description of a child destined for greatness. In fact it looks like a grim situation, one in which average would be welcomed, but not for Debbie Phelps. As a teacher, Debbie was determined she would help her son find success. "I knew that, if I collaborated with Michael, he could achieve anything he set his mind to," she said.[17]

By twelve Michael was still struggling in school but was swimming two to three hours daily and getting up at 6:30 a.m. for morning practice. Debbie realized that swimming was her son's key to greatness. She used his love of the pool to help in the classroom. She encouraged his math tutor to use swimming word problems. When he struggled in reading she encouraged him to read the sports section of the newspaper.

But Debbie did more than just help her son to focus on school-work. She recalled one swim meet when in frustration Michael pulled off his goggles and threw them onto the deck. On the way home they talked about the value of sportsmanship. She told him that sportsmanship counted as much as winning. "We came up with a signal I could give him from the stands," she says. "I'd form a 'C' with my hand, which stood for 'compose yourself.' Every time I saw him getting frustrated, I'd give him the sign. Once, he gave me the 'C' when I got stressed while making dinner. You never know what's sinking in until the tables are turned!"[18]

Debbie Phelps is a great example of a mother who fought to see her child meet his potential. She overcame negative comments, disgruntled teachers, divorce, and ADHD. She wanted Michael to be confident and to learn. Through her help he went on to attend college and become the most decorated Olympic athlete of all time.

The Push

According to Psalm 139 and 2 Peter 1:3, God has designed us and given us everything we need to live our physical and spiritual lives. He then placed us in the right atmosphere so we could develop into the person He has called us to be. He allows trials, difficulties, and even temptation to enter our lives because each ingredient molds us into His image. But knowing all this, all of us still need a push every now and then.

Mothers are pushers. They are the ones who encourage and inspire greatness from each of their children. As a mother, it's your job to use the intuition God gave you to push your children in the right direction.

I like to think of the push as a combination of belief and courage. When someone believes in you and sees with the eyes of faith what you can become, he pushes you to do more than you thought you could. Pushers refuse to let you settle for ordinary when you have more in you to give. They instill confidence into your spirit so that you have courage to take that next step. And that next step is often the difference between average and above average.

It takes a special touch to be a pusher. Pushing is not about hurting or scaring someone. It's not about maintaining a high level of intensity and driving a person into the ground. Pushing is all about encouragement. It's finding ways to encourage your children to take one more step, to try one more time, and to overcome their own self-defeating behaviors.

As a coach and a teacher, my job was pushing. Every team I have coached had players who thought they were "God's gift to basketball" and those who thought they had to settle for average. Each year my classes were filled with students whose highest aspirations were to pass the class. Through the years I have learned that what makes a player great is not skill alone. The difference between a "C" student and a "B" student is not always intelligence. Attitude makes the difference, and attitudes are developed along the way as we respond to life.

We will all make mistakes along the way and each of us have areas that are not our strengths, but how we respond to these mistakes and weaknesses is what makes the difference. Sometimes our children will want to quit. Other times they will beat themselves up and be afraid to risk again. It's at these times they need a mother's push. I know that pushing can sometimes be scary, so I will share a little coaching tip with you. Take what you have learned about being a good parent and combine that with your instinctive know-how and you will become a great pusher.

Carol Burnett has always been one of my favorite comedic actresses. In her book *One More Time*, she tells the story of an encourager who changed her life. While Carol was a student at UCLA, a man came to her and asked her what she wanted to do with her life. She quickly told him that her goal was to get to New York and start a career in musical theatre. He asked her why she wanted to do that. Her reply was simple, "Because I will never be happy doing anything else." That day the man handed Carol a thousand dollars and told her that the money had a few stipulations: it had to be used to go to New York; she could not tell anyone who gave her the money; and she had to promise to help other people out along the way, just as he had helped her. She agreed and the rest is history. Carol Burnett went on to become an icon in the industry, and according to those who know her well, she spent her career helping others who were just getting started.[19]

Carol Burnett and thousands of others who we will never hear about have had the necessary ingredients for success: a push and a "can do" attitude. Although many people are born with a positive attitude, eventually life has a way zapping it out of them. I meet many young people who are so scared of failure they refuse to try. I meet others who are so apathetic that it seems they have no direction or goal for their lives. Our children need to know that God has a special purpose for their lives and that we believe they can accomplish this purpose. Help your children dream big. Help them find God's direction for their lives. Pour courage into them, and every now and again give them a push in the right direction.

Part Three

My Mama's Standing Guard

❦

Chapter 11

New Recruits

From Toddler to Tween

When new recruits join the military, they go through intense training in order to earn their rank and title. There is much to learn before they can earn their stripes, and as far as the military is concerned, they have to earn the right to be a soldier. They have to prove their willingness to work hard, do the job right, and endure the intense training. As they move up through the ranks their status changes and they earn stripes, bars, and other insignia to add to their uniform. This lets others know who they are and what they have accomplished at just a glance.

Our children all start out just like new recruits. They are young and everything is new to them. They have much to learn about surviving in the world. From the very beginning parents teach them the skills they need and watch as they earn their stripes.

In this chapter, we'll look at some of the common stages all children go through as they grow and develop. First we'll take a quick look at the developmental stages from infancy to age twelve, then we'll take a closer look at the new "tween" phenomenon.

Infant to Age Two

Prior to two years old, children need to learn that they can trust their parents to take care of them and to love them. Parents meet this need by feeding them, providing a roof over their heads, and demonstrating their love through hugs, kisses, and cuddling. Children who are mistreated or neglected at this age will struggle with security issues and will fail to trust others as they should. Although there are many children in this world who are neglected at this age, I find that most parents love the early days with their children. They love holding them and watching them try new things as they learn about life and as they grow.

Two to Four Years Old

As a child reaches the age between eighteen months and two years old, he reaches the second step. In this stage children learn about thinking and feeling. For the first time in their lives they are able to do some things for themselves. This is a great feeling for a small child. They want to do everything "all by myself." As a parent you cannot let them do as much as they would like, so it's important to find a platform for their creativity and their newfound drive to do it themselves. Let them try to do as many things as is safely possible. Be patient as you teach them the correct way to do things. Remember that at this age they are copycats and they will learn much faster by watching what you do.

As they move through this stage they will either feel successful in their attempts and gain more confidence or they will be embarrassed that they can't do anything right. I have watched so many children at this age go into a fit of anger when they can't seem to get something right or when they are not allowed to do something. I often wonder when I watch these tantrums unfold whether their parents are giving them opportunities to feel in control of any area of their life. You can still be the parent and yet allow your child to exert some control over her life. Children at this age are going to spill milk, make a mess with their spaghetti, and take a long time to climb the stairs. But allowing them the opportunity to feed themselves and hold the cup and climb the steps gives them the confidence they need to accomplish the next big step. They should not be allowed to be disrespectful or to disobey, but parents must not frustrate a child's desire to try things on her own.

Play Age: Four to Six Years Old

Children in this age group are so much fun. Their imagination switch is flipped on and they experience life in a whole new way. They play games, make friends, and begin to understand that people are different. They also begin to desire more responsibility. Most children will start school sometime during this age. As they enter school they don't want to be treated like a baby anymore. Although they still may want you to hold them and fix their boo-boos, they don't want you to make a fuss in front of their new friends.

At this age children will begin to ask many questions about God, and you should encourage their new hunger for knowledge. Be faithful to teach your children about God and about how much He loves them. Share with them what Christ did for us on the cross. Make sure they have a clear understanding of sin, forgiveness, and what trusting Christ is all about. You can usually find out if they understand by asking them questions that require more than a "yes" or "no." Be patient and let the Holy Spirit do His work in their lives.

As preschoolers try to take initiative, encourage them. There are many positive activities that you can get them involved in at this age. This is a great time for swimming lessons, t-ball, soccer, ballet, and gymnastics. Encouraging your children to be physically active in a non-competitive way is a great outlet for their energy and positive reinforcement as they learn to cooperate with others.

Elementary School Years: Ages Six to Twelve

During this wide age span children make incredible changes physically, emotionally, mentally, and socially. It is hard to keep up with them from month to month as they change. School is the impetus for so many of these changes. As children grow they are capable of learning and accomplishing many new skills. These new skills can either make them feel industrious and capable of doing more or inferior and lacking.

Up to this point, the playing field has been relatively even for everyone. Suddenly the influx of grades, reading groups, and accelerated programs divide children into academic groups. Clothes, tennis shoes, lunches, backpacks, and gadgets divide children into economic groups. And social groups separate the accepted from the unaccepted. All the kids in school recognize these groups, and they can easily become the structure kids build their life around.

Children of this age are learning to adapt to structure, and parents must develop the home as the primary source of that structure. Since school is often such an unstable environment, the home needs to be a place of stability. Consistency is vital. Children need to know where the lines are drawn, and will try their limits to see where the lines are drawn when it come to rules and responsibilities. This is not an act of rebellion but of learning.

Mom, this is not the time for you to be indecisive about what direction you are going. Both parents should be clear on what behavior is acceptable and what is unacceptable. Don't make your child guess or experiment to find the lines. Be open and upfront in communicating what you expect from her. If the line is constantly moving, she will push you every time. If you are unsure where to draw the line for certain things, start with the strictest approach. As a young teacher I learned quickly that it is easier to let up than to tighten up.

As children grow, parents should help develop their industriousness by providing them with responsibility at home to give them a sense of ownership and duty to the family. When they are young their jobs may be small, but they should be recognized as important. As they grow older their duties should increase. This should increase their dependability.

Once your children learn what they are responsible for and what they are responsible to do, things will run much smoother. They need to understand that their actions have consequences and they are responsible for their own actions. You should not have to spend thirty minutes arguing with them about their bedtime or their household chores. They should be expected to do the right thing, and when they don't you will need to provide consistent consequences every time. Over time they will learn that in order to change the reaction, they must change the action.

Who Are the Tweens?

Tween is the marketing buzzword for children between the ages of eight and twelve. They are not yet teenagers, but in so many ways they are more teen than child. It seems that someone has magically moved the scale of childhood backwards. The twelve-year-olds of yesterday are the ten-year-olds of today. It's as if someone flips a switch and your little girl is suddenly taking down her poster of cute puppies and replacing it with the latest heartthrob. Marketing VOX, a company that specializes in online marketing, explains the gap between the physical and social development of tweens: "While they are physically still children, socially they are beginning to explore what it means to be a teenager—a state they think is typified by freedoms they lack."[20]

Tweens want to feel grown up, and much of their lifestyle is allowing them to achieve this. One-third of tweens have their own mobile phone.[21] They have a large market geared to supplying anything and everything for their specific needs. As they leave their childishness behind and search for more freedom and more power, you need to recognize the changes and be a part of making this transition as smooth as possible.

Absentee Parents

Kay Hymowitz, author of *Liberation's Children: Parents and Kids in a Postmodern Age*, writes that the causes for tween's behavior is complex but that two major themes revealed themselves as she talked to educators and child psychologists: "a sexualized and glitzy media-driven marketplace and absentee parents."[22] Hymowitz goes on to say that "what has been less commonly recognized is at this age, the two causes combine to augment the authority of the peer group, which in turn both weakens the influence of parents and reinforces the power of the media. Taken together, parental absence, the market, and the peer group form a vicious circle that works to distort the development of youngsters."[23]

Are you an absentee parent? I am sure you feel as if you are there for your children. But the question still must be asked, "Are you really?" Being present and being active are two very different things.

I know many mothers who are present. They do all the "mommy" things. They feed their kids, help them with homework, and shuttle them to activities. But do they actively engage their children? Do they connect with them and communicate with them? Are they on the lookout for problems and actively addressing any issues that come up? Believe it or not, it's possible to be a stay-at-home mom and still neglect your child's deepest spiritual and emotional needs.

Because the early years of parenting are so physically intense, it can often be a big sigh of relief when your children are mature enough to handle the little things on their own. For most mothers, their children's independence is a big help. Mothers are often willing to allow their child to throw a meal in the microwave, hang out at a friend's house after school, or come home to an empty house. It's not that any of these things are wrong, but together they add up to children spending more time alone and less time interacting with the right influences. There is a tradeoff, and that tradeoff is a valuable connection with your child. Your influence is not optional if your children are going to establish moral values and personal identity. The tween years are not the time for parents to relax but to engage at an even higher level.

Media and Your Tween

Because media has such an influence over tweens, moms will need to monitor movies, magazines, music, websites, and television. Your tween will not be interested in kids' shows anymore. They will be interested in media that is "hot." What is "hot" changes about as often as the term itself, but over the years the tween age group has proved to the industry that it has an impact on what sells. Since the late eighties this age group has proved they can launch a singing group or a movie to number one. The overwhelming success of the movie *Titanic* can be credited in part to tween girls who just couldn't get enough of Leonardo de Caprio. The kids of *High School Musical* have tweens to thank for their success as well. Singing groups from *New Kids on the Block* to the *Jonas Brothers* have tween girls to thank for their chart-topping success. Magazines such as *Cosmopolitan*

Girl have seen success due to the desire of tween girls to be fashion savvy. *Nickelodeon* has found great success by tapping into this age group with television shows, movies, and a new generation of cartoons. *SpongeBob* and the *Naked Brothers Band* lead the way for music, style, and much more.

Sadly enough the media industry is much more aware than parents of what tweens like. As I talk to mothers, I find they do not really know what their children are interested in. They have heard the celebrities' names but have not taken the time to find out who they are and what message they are sending. It seems parents have taken an "all or nothing" position when it comes to media choices. It's easier to say "no" with no explanation than to take the time to check it out. Or it's easier to say "yes" with no restrictions if you don't want the argument and you aren't going to take the time to check it out. We need mothers who are willing to find out who their children are listening to and what they are watching. Then sit down and make a thoughtful choice that is best for your child. Be willing to explain to them the reasons behind your decision.

The Internet

As you monitor your children's media choices, don't forget the computer. This technology has opened up our world in new and amazing ways, but the devil has also used it to bring evil closer to home. Gone are the days when a young man had to sneak around to buy a dirty magazine and keep it hidden in his room. Today pornography is at his fingertips through the computer keyboard.

It's a crazy world out there, but I don't think the answer is to refuse to allow your kids to use the computer. In today's world computer skills are a must for survival. So what is the answer? I believe informed parents are the first line of defense for their children in cyberspace.

There are three easy steps parents should take to keep their children safe online. First, keep all computers in public areas of the house. Kids do not need computers in their rooms. Secular agencies suggest this as one of the best preventives, but Christian parents seem shocked when I suggest it. One mother even bemoaned the fact that she'd just had her kitchen and den remodeled and didn't want to tacky it up with computer wires and printers. She had moved the computer to the basement, and her son's computer activity had doubled. She was wondering what he was doing, but the thought of those wires really had her in a dilemma.

I know computer wires are ugly, but you have to put your priorities in order. Your children's future may depend on it. Boys need the accountability of a public room so they can make the right decisions online. Boys are targeted by the pornography industry. It's easy to come up on the wrong thing while surfing. They don't need the temptation that privacy affords them. Make it a policy at your home that all computer use happens in a central location.

The second easy step for parents is to go to www.bsafehome. com and install the Bsafe Internet filter on all your computers. I can't begin to tell you all the wonderful things this filter will do for you. It monitors all chat room activity, logs instant messages and e-mails, has a spam filter and a pop-up blocker, filters all adult content, and allows you to customize your list of allowed websites. When your children understand that you will get a report each week of their activity on the web, that you can look at their conversations online if you need to, and that you have access to their passwords, you will give them much-needed supervision and accountability.

Lastly, teach your children how to be smart on social networking sites such as MySpace and Facebook. Young people love to connect with their friends online and share pictures, videos, and what is on their minds. Unfortunately, many of them are oblivious to the dangers of these sites. Here are a few simple instructions they can use to protect themselves and have fun while keeping up with their friends.

First of all, make sure they set all their accounts to private so no one can access them without permission. Second, they should never give out personal information like phone numbers and addresses. Last, I encourage you to set up your own account and become one of your child's online friends. This will help you become proactive in protecting your child online.

Tween Girls and Fashion

Clothing can become a huge source of contention during this age because many tween girls want to dress like adults and have a sophisticated look. Teachers frequently share with me their struggle with tween girls as they come to school with streaked hair, high heels, and makeup. I agonize as I see ten-year-old girls in shirts that are midriff revealing and skirts that are way too short. Our little girls are accelerating into a world that they do not understand and that they are not mature enough for. Why? Robert L. Johnson, director of adolescent and young-adult medicine at the University of Medicine and Dentistry of New Jersey, feels he knows the answer. "Kids wear sexually provocative clothes at nine because their parents buy them provocative clothes, not because of their hormones."[24]

Moms, did you hear that? *You* are responsible for how your tween girl dresses. I know you feel the pressure from your daughter to buy her trendy clothes. But there is a difference between trendy and provocative. If the style is sexy, then eleven-year-old girls do not need to own it. Trust me when I tell you that behavior follows closely behind their wardrobe. When they dress sexy or flirtatious, they have the desire to act upon the feelings that those outfits give them.

What concerns me the most is how many parents are failing to see the problems. Mothers want their girls to stay pure but see no problem with letting them dress to attract attention. I have heard every excuse from fear of tantrums, avoiding teenage rebellion, and finding nothing else to buy. Moms, there is no excuse if you want to raise a battle-ready girl.

Many of the parents I talk with are concerned about makeup and clothes but feel there is no way to beat the media and the fashion industry. There is hope, but you have to get in early and make your presence felt in her life. She needs to know that you want her to be nicely dressed but not at the expense of modesty and reputation. Help her make adjustments. Taking her shopping is an important part of the process, but make sure she understands the guidelines before you enter the mall. This will help you avoid the emotional standoffs that end with a miserable mother and daughter and no purchases. Be creative. Certain tops would work if you bought a larger size.

Layering is always a helpful tool as well. But even the most creative mother will have to draw the line and say "no" to clothing that is too provocative. Give your daughter the confidence to be a trendsetter for the right look.

Be a Leader

Lead your children through this bumpy transition time. It may not always be easy to start conversations regarding sensitive subjects with your preteen, but if you don't, someone else will. Set your heart and mind to the task of raising children who can think and act in a manner that would please God and bring joy to their lives.

Time passes so fast. You hardly blink and that toddler is suddenly ten years old and already talking about being a teenager. These years are so important for building their foundation. The lessons you teach them and the habits that you instill in them during this period will last for a lifetime. Come on, moms! This is not the time to sit back and let their peers, their coach, or the media train your children. Put on your combat boots and begin to direct the placement of the material going into your child's life. You will be glad you did.

Chapter 12

G.I. Jane

Raising Your Daughter

In 1775 women served in the American Revolution as nurses, cooks, and aides. In 1866 Dr. Mary Walker received the Medal of Honor for her contribution to the Civil War. In World War I more than 21,000 women served as nurses on battlefields and in hospitals. Women were telephone operators, stenographers, and clerks in every branch of the U.S. military. By World War II women were flying airplanes, working in intelligence, and some were even captured by the Japanese and held as POWs. By Operation Desert Storm, some 40,000 American military women were deployed and sent to fight for our country. Today many women are serving in some capacity in our military and many are in Iraq and Afghanistan fighting the war against terror.[25]

Women serving in the military is a very debated topic because women are so different than men. Regardless of what you think about this issue, you have to admit that God made boys and girls differently. He not only made them different physically, but he also gave them different strengths and weaknesses and different ways of thinking and processing information. This diversity between the sexes makes them a great combination when they work together because they both have much to offer.

Same, Yet Different

In the amazing creation account of Genesis, God created man and put him in charge of all the creatures. But Adam was still alone — none of the creatures were suitable helpers or companions for him. So God took a rib from man and formed a woman. Adam took one look and knew this was the companion he needed, bone of his bones and flesh of his flesh. Both Adam and Eve were made in the image of God and declared good, but they looked and acted very differently.

As science has progressed in uncovering the mysteries of the universe, we have begun to understand just how different the sexes actually are. Men pump more blood through their veins, while women have fewer red blood cells. This gives men a great capacity for oxygen allowing them more energy and endurance. Men's bodies are twice as muscular as women's. But despite the apparent physical edge, women outlive men by more than eight years. Women age slower and tend to keep their mental capacities longer. Women are built different and are hormonally different than men in every way.

We know that God loves both men and women, and in many ways they are the same. Christ died for both, both have sinned, both have the capacity to love and to need others, both have strengths and weaknesses, but despite a long list of similarities, men and women are different. One sex is not better than the other and God does not love one more than the other, but just as He does all creation, He treats them in accordance to their design.

The sex of your children will affect them physically, mentally, and emotionally. In this chapter and the next, I will highlight some of the issues unique to each gender, especially those issues that today's moms need to understand and address.

Sugar and Spice and Everything Nice

Girls are great. Since I am one that makes me a little partial, but there are so many wonderful things about being a woman. As a young girl, though, I couldn't imagine what any of those would be, because I was a tomboy. I loved athletics and the outdoors. My younger brothers and I spent most of our early childhood building forts, playing in the woods, riding our bicycles through the neighborhood, and playing whatever sport was in season. When I went to school and recess time came, all the girls would run for the swings, but I played pick-up games with the guys. I couldn't see anything cool about being a girl.

Of course time has a way of changing things. As I grew older I began to see that being a girl wasn't so bad after all. God brought some wonderful people into my life during my formative years who modeled what it meant to be a great woman. Nancy Reilly was one of those women. Nancy was one of the prettiest women I had ever seen, classy and sharp in the way she dressed and conducted herself. She was married to Ron Reilly, an evangelist who also had an impact on my life. Sometimes she would come to summer camp with her husband Ron and have special sessions just for girls. I remember sitting there listening to her and thinking that if I could be half as cool as she was, being a girl might not be all that bad.

I often think of Nancy as I get ready to go out and speak to young girls. I remember how much her influence impacted my life, and I pray that God would allow something about my life to have that same impact on the girls listening to me.

Although I still hate the drama and all the weeping, I love being a girl. I love chick flicks, shopping till I drop, handbags, shoes—oh, especially shoes—and things that smell nice and things that are soft. But I still love almost any sport. I love to hike in the mountains, snorkel off a reef, and I still love to beat my brothers at anything. Through the years God showed me that He made me unique. I am a girl, but I am not like any other girl on the planet. He made me just right for His purpose in my life.

It took me a while to come to believe that as strongly as I do today. There were days I wondered why I had been given my dad's muscular football build, especially when my brother was drinking protein drinks and working out for several hours a day to try and "buff up." I would have gladly given him my body as long as I could have his long legs, perfect complexion, and inability to gain weight. But God didn't make a mistake. He knew exactly what I needed to be like to fulfill His will for my life.

Bodies and Beauty

Today's girls need to know that God made each of us different but good. It's tough out there. There is pressure from every side to be on what I call the "A list." To be on the "A list," you have to be popular, you have to be a part of the "in" crowd, you have to have a cute figure, you can't be overweight, you have to be liked by the boys, and you have to have at least one of them who is crazy about you. Many girls will do almost anything to get on the "A list." Some of them puke in toilets after they eat a meal, some of them take laxatives, some of them work out obsessively, and some just starve themselves. Others make sure their thong is showing, allow boys to grope them, and go all the way.

The pressure of our culture's skewed view of beauty is affecting girls and women alike. It makes us hate the way God made us and spend our lives trying to change it. Nothing is ever good enough. The requirements are mind-boggling. Women are required to be small in some areas and big in others but not too big or too small. No pressure—perfection is all it demands. Our girls watch movies and look at women on the front covers of their favorite magazines or online and think that it's all real. It's not! It takes makeup artists, hair stylists, lighting specialists, professional photographers, and designer clothes to pull off one photo, and even that shot is not good enough. Then that photo has to be enhanced by a computer. By the time it hits the front cover, there is not much real about it. Blemishes are removed; everything is perfect. That is just not how we are—not Hollywood, and not the average girl. Women spend most of their lives trying to be something that doesn't exist. It's wrong and it's damaging.

There is not a perfect size for all girls. There is not a perfect hair color. Your daughter needs to understand that her perfect size and hair color is not up to her. Just because she is not a size four doesn't mean that she is unacceptable. A girl's self-concept will go with her for a lifetime, so she will need to develop a healthy image of herself and who God made her to be at an early age.

A mother is such an important part of this equation. As girls enter their teenage years, their self-image will be tested and how they really feel about themselves will be revealed. This is where you come in—your job is to help her see her real worth through the lens of God's Word and to see that what the world defines as "hot" is just smoke and mirrors.

Because of the overemphasis on looks in our society, many young women have adopted the wrong attitudes about their bodies, reducing them to feeling like objects for boys to look at and touch. Girls who don't have a boyfriend consider themselves second-class citizens. I have had heartbreaking conversations with girls who describe the lengths they are going to keep a guy in their lives. One young girl shared with me how her sixteen-year-old boyfriend slapped her and shoved her around. Tears streamed down her face as she looked at me and asked what she should do.

I was a little stunned the first time I was asked this question. What do you do? Was she really confused about that? You walk away! That is what you do! I will never forget the look she gave me as she mumbled these words in reply, "But then I wouldn't have a boyfriend." It wouldn't be the last time some girl would hang around after a session to ask me that question.

Mothers have to realize how important their daughter's definition of beauty is to her development of confidence. Moms have to help their daughters through these important life lessons. If your girl is going to survive today's culture with a healthy image of herself and the confidence to build positive relationships, she must get it straight in her head and in her heart.

I know it's hard for many mothers to talk to their daughters about these issues because they also battle some of the same things. Women in their forties and fifties still struggle with staying on the "A list." Plastic surgery and beauty enhancement is a billion-dollar business thanks to so many confused, self-conscious women. I am all for looking pretty, and if you can afford the treatments and feel you need some help, then go ahead. But many women turn to plastic surgery and beauty enhancements because they feel they must turn back time or be ruined. They fear their husbands will leave them for a younger model if they don't make the changes. Their insecurities drive them to a place where nothing can satisfy.

You must address the issue of self-image with your daughter so that she isn't caught up in this vicious cycle, because it doesn't stop when you are twenty. Self-image continues becoming a bigger monster the older you get. It affects your relationship with your friends, with your husband, and with the world around you.

Women often struggle with feelings of inadequacy, comparing themselves to other women and getting depressed when they feel they don't measure up. If you struggle with feelings of inadequacy, you can only imagine how difficult it will be for your daughter when she reaches your age. It's time women of all ages realize that beauty is not something conjured up by makeovers and potions. Beauty is not about what you weigh or what you wear. Beauty is what comes from the heart and overflows into the life.

One of the things I have learned and am still working on in my own life is the fact that God is still working to make me a better me. I used to think that as God was working on me He was making me into someone else. I would pray that God would make me cute and skinny like Meg Ryan. I would read passages of Scripture where women were praised for being quiet and I would try to go for a full day and be quiet. It never worked. People thought something was wrong with me and asked me if I was sick. What I didn't understand is that God is not making me into someone else—He is making me into a better me. He loves me just the way I am, and in His eyes I am beautiful. Realizing this helped me to grasp that I didn't need a boyfriend to be accepted. I was already accepted by the Person who knew me best and loved me most, Jesus. I didn't need to be on the "A list" or look like Meg Ryan. I could relax and be the person it was easiest for me to be—myself!

Even today this thought keeps me steady in my relationships and reminds me of what is worthy of my time and energy. As I grow older and see more wrinkles in the mirror and more grey hair in my brush, I know that I can rest in the confidence I have in Christ. My hairstylist can help me with the grey and Oil of Olay can help me with the wrinkles, but only God can make me beautiful.

Being Comfortable in Your Own Skin

So much of life for women can be about competition if we are not careful—competition for the best grades, the trendiest clothes, the cutest boyfriend. Don't let your daughters get caught up in the world of jealousy and comparing. A woman who is confident in who God has made her is also free to allow others to be themselves.

As girls grow into womanhood, they will learn to build relationships or to destroy them. Feelings of inadequacy and jealousy can cause a woman to do evil things. Women who have all the potential to be sweet, kind, beautiful, understanding, and gracious can also be vindictive, hateful, conniving, and destructive. Women who view other women as competition to be analyzed and destroyed will only hurt others.

The devil wants women to self-destruct. He knows that if he can get little girls to struggle with feelings of jealousy, strife, and hatred, he has a great head start. Remember elementary school? It starts with making fun of people who don't fit your mold, ugly words, and notes passed in class. It grows to exclusive clubs and groups that only allow certain people in. It's displayed in arrogance, haughtiness, pride, and self-absorption. The monster continues to grow through each grade level until it becomes a way of thinking that permeates your character. It doesn't end at adulthood but only becomes more sophisticated. Each step is another chain to a life of bondage.

Paul warns us against this behavior. "But if you bite and devour one another, take care that you are not consumed by one another" (Galatians 5:15 NASB). Paul gives a long list of actions and attitudes that are part of the flesh. Jealousy, dissensions, and envy are among that list. He reminds us that as Christians we are not subject to these behaviors because we have the Spirit living within us. If we live in a fleshly pattern, it is because we choose to be bound to that lifestyle and thought pattern, not because we have no choice. The Spirit desires for us to bear His fruit in our lives, which will enable us to love others, to be joyful, peaceful, patient, and kind. This fruit will produce kindness and goodness in our hearts and lives. God has called us to love, not to compete.

Our girls need to understand they have nothing to prove to anyone. They do not have to compete with other girls for their place in life.

Putting others down does not make you look better. What people say about you is not who you are. Kids can be cruel. Nicknames can linger in a person's mind forever. Whoever said "Sticks and stones may break my bones but words will never hurt me" had never been hit by a word. Words are powerful and they have the power to label a person for life. It is amazing what you accept as truth when you hear it enough. That is why it is so important for you to help your daughter realize that God loves her, you love her, and that she matters to you and God. This reinforcement will give her value, and when she feels valuable as a person, she will have hope. If your daughter has been one of those who has been bullied and teased most of her life, this realization will start the healing process for her. It will help her to see that she can rise above and stand up for herself. In confidence she can know that God highly values her just as she is.

One of my favorite verses in Scripture is Isaiah 41:9–10. These are great verses to share with your daughter as she learns to be comfortable in her own skin.

> Thou art my servant; I have chosen thee, and not cast thee away. Fear thou not; for I am with thee: be not dismayed; for I am thy God: I will strengthen thee: yea, I will help thee; yea, I will uphold thee with the right hand of my righteousness.

All for the Glory of God

If your daughter is on the "A list", keep a close eye on her attitude. Teach her early that nothing about her makes her better than someone else. God gave us our looks, our intelligence, our talents, and our abilities. It is up to us to use those things for His glory.

Kelley Glascock Robison has been a friend of mine for a long time. I met her when she was just fifteen years old. Kelley is beautiful, one of those girls that God has blessed with gorgeous features. In high school, she was definitely on the "A list"—a cheerleader, a ball player, popular, and talented in music. I met Kelley when I was coaching college volleyball. She attended the summer camp program that we offered, and throughout the year I scouted her games. Kelley was a good player and I was prepared to offer her a scholarship to play volleyball when she reached her senior year, but God had other plans for Kelley.

During the summer, Kelley's youth group went on a fun activity to a church member's house on the lake. Some of the kids jumped in a few boats and headed out on the lake to water ski. Kelley had been swimming and was bobbing in the water when she was hit by another boat, whose driver did not see Kelley. Kelley's leg was cut off at the knee by the boat's propeller. For weeks Kelley was in the ICU clinging to life. She finally gained enough strength to start the long process of surgeries and learning to walk again.

I kept up with Kelley's progress and before long she was rolling into one of my practices in her wheelchair. I could tell by the determined look on her face that day that this wasn't the end for her. Before long Kelley was walking on her new leg. She graduated from high school, and four years later returned home from college with another diploma in hand. If you visit my church on any given Sunday you will find her playing the keyboard. She also teaches a women's aerobic class on Tuesday nights. She is married to a wonderful young man and has two delightful children.

When Kelley walks on stage to give her testimony to teens they never notice her slight limp. In fact, the kids' heads snap up when she tells them about her accident. They strain over the crowd to see and seem genuinely shocked at her story. From that point on, Kelley has them in the palm of her hand as she tells them what God taught her through it all.

Kelley admits that she became consumed with life on the "A list". She confesses that she knew what God had given her and she flaunted it. You could hear a pin drop as she shares how God has taught her that life is not about being on the "A list". Life is about people. Life is about loving people despite their differences. Life is about putting God first and not being in competition with everyone around you. Pleasing God is what is important. Silence hangs in the air as Kelley finishes, and then suddenly from all across the building kids stand to their feet and with thunderous applause let Kelley know that they have heard her words.

Our girls need to know that they are at their best when they are themselves. Help your daughter to be comfortable in her own skin. Teach her that she is precious to God and to you. God has something for her to do, and through His power she can do great things. The sky is the limit for our girls if they will stop comparing and competing. When they start loving and caring about others, they give everyone around them a glimpse of their beauty and grace. When people see a heart full of love and compassion for other people, a heart that is not jealous and refuses to compete, a heart that rejoices in the success of others and is kind, then they will see the true beauty that lies within.

Girls who understand what it truly means to be beautiful will find comfort and confidence in being themselves. As they grow comfortable in their own skin and learn to relax, certain concepts will become clear to them. They will not struggle as much with modesty because they understand its value. Society will not control their view of themselves or the world around them. They will not need to sacrifice their morals to get a boyfriend. They will learn that if they follow God, He will guide them and bless them.

Help your daughter find herself. Take her to Psalm 139 and let her see that God designed her for a purpose and according to Him she is wonderfully made. Show her what it is like to be a woman who has found the balance between outward beauty and inward beauty. Teach her that true modesty is an issue of the heart not the hem. If this is her foundation, I believe she will grow up to be a beautiful woman of God.

Chapter 13

G.I. Joe

Raising Your Son

❧

In 1964, Hasbro, the toy company, designed a twelve-inch action figure named G.I. Joe. The G.I. stood for "Government Issued" and had become a generic term for U.S. soldiers. The toy became a hit among little boys. In fact, I remember playing with my brothers' G.I. Joe when I was just a kid. (He married Barbie on several occasions.) Today G.I. Joe is still alive and well. He is in the movies and there is still a line of action figures with a full array of vehicles, artillery, and clothing. G.I. Joe has been the ultimate boy action figure for more than forty years because he represents the things that boys love.

Enter a room full of little boys and you have entered a room full of sword fights, car noises, and in most cases, high energy. They make guns out of pencils and race around shooting each other, hitting the floor in great drama at their demise, and then they are right back up to play again. Hit the playground and you find them huddled in groups playing hard and keeping score.

Boys at Risk?

Boys are fun, they are carefree, but they are at risk. In today's society boys seem to be unsure of themselves and where they are headed. Many of them are doing poorly in school and are more likely to fall prey to violence, alcohol, and drugs. Many boys float about unsure of themselves, unsure of relationships, and unwilling to communicate what is going on inside their heads and hearts.

For many years psychologists and educators tried to convince parents that boys and girls were just the same. Teachers couldn't make it work in a classroom, and parents were having no luck at home. Despite the propaganda, we have come full circle. New research is supporting what we already knew: boys and girls are different, and that is a good thing. God created two unique individuals when He created man and woman. They have different roles, different responsibilities, and different ways of thinking.

God's Word also shows us that even in the male gender, each male has his own individual qualities. I think no example could be more striking than that of Jacob and Esau. Esau was described as a red, hairy guy who liked to hunt. Jacob was described as a smooth-skinned, fair guy who liked to hang out around the tents and cook. At first read you might think that Jacob was just a mama's boy who was a little on the soft side. But as you continue to read about their lives you will find that Jacob was strong enough to move a rock that usually took many men to move, and he spent a long night wrestling with God. He was so determined that God took his hip out of joint so he would stop. That doesn't sound like too much of a sissy to me. Jacob and Esau were just different, even though they were twins.

Boys develop differently than girls and are affected by male hormones in very different ways. While girls tend to start socializing at very young ages, boys tend to be less talkative and struggle with communication skills more than girls. It has been said that girls use more adjectives in a day than boys use words. If you have ever struggled talking to your young man, then you probably understand this exaggeration.

Developmental Stages for Boys

As their mother you have the wonderful opportunity to help your boys become men. There are three basic stages for boys, according to Steve Biddulph, author of *Raising Boys*.[26] The first stage is from birth to six. At this age, boys really belong to their mothers. Dads play a large role, but at this age, Mom gives them love and security.

From age six to fourteen, boys start desiring to become a man. Something inside of them pushes them to be masculine, and during this time they look to their father. They want to learn how to be like him, so they need him to take an interest in their lives and become involved in their daily activities. Although their mothers will still be very involved in their lives, their fathers will help them build competence and confidence in who they are as a male.

Finally they enter the last stage, from age fourteen to adulthood. At this stage boys tend to need their mom and dad a little less and look to male mentors to give them direction. If their parents don't organize some good role models during this time, their sons will turn to their friends to help them navigate these unpredictable years. Youth pastors, coaches, teachers, and grandfathers have the opportunity to assist you as a parent. As you place positive role models in the lives of your boys, you will find they gain a positive sense of who they are and how they are a part of the world around them.

Biddulph's stages do not mean that moms are out of the picture from six years old on. Mothers continue to play an active role in the lives of their boys, encouraging, training, and loving. Moms have a unique connection with their sons that is very important to their emotional development, their ability to communicate, and their ability to establish meaningful relationships.

An Uphill Battle?

As a mother you may feel as if you are fighting an uphill battle with your boys. For years mothers have wondered why their boys never listen, can't seem to obey, and tend to jump off of everything. Understanding that these issues are part of their uniqueness as a male will you help you find creative ways to harness that energy into positive outcomes. We cannot treat boys like girls and expect them to behave and respond in the same way.

Medical research is beginning to help us see into the world of boys. Because boys tend to have more energy than girls, they are more likely to be diagnosed with a "disorder," such as hyperactivity, attention deficit, or oppositional defiant behavior. Although boys tend to struggle with ADHD and other issues like this more frequently than girls, many boys are being labeled because they are misunderstood. Boys are full of energy, and the male hormone testosterone affects their bodies in such a way that they need to be on the go. They need outlets where they can get out, run, and burn off some of that energy. Just as recess is important in school, it is also important that parents find energy outlets for their boys at home. You can't expect them to stay in the house all day and play quietly in their rooms. Outdoor playtime is important for boys because this is a place where they can be a little wild and destructive and yet not get into trouble.

Boys do not hear as well as girls. Many times they don't listen to you simply because they didn't hear you. If you think your son is struggling in this area, inform his teacher so he can sit closer to the front of the room. Make sure you are close to him when you are giving him instructions. Yelling instructions up the stairs may be more convenient, but many times he may not understand half of what you have said.

Boys' brains are different. Boys have more of their brain area dedicated to mechanical and logical functioning than verbal and emotional functioning. So, for example, they enjoy moving things through the air, such as balls or airplanes, but they can't tell you why they are feeling down as easily as girls do. When boys are stressed they tend to choose seclusion. If you see your son pull away, you may want to pay more attention to what could be causing him anxiety.

Boys are more likely to engage in dangerous activities. Risky behavior doesn't bother most of them at all. The adrenaline rush they get from attempting dangerous things makes the whole experience even more appealing. So if you have a boy who likes to climb up to the top of your cabinets, the closet, or the tallest tree in your yard and doesn't seem to notice the danger, now you know why. Boys are drawn to skateboards, popping wheelies on their bicycles, motorbikes, and aggressive sports. This is why they will need to be supervised more to reduce injury.

Boys also compartmentalize and structure their learning. Girls tend to make many connections from all areas of their brain, but boys think differently. They have less blood flow to their brains, so they keep things more structured and less connected. This biological fact helps us understand why boys need structure in their lives. Boys are looking for organization, and if no one is leading, they will set up their own leadership structure. This is why we find so many gangs in our inner cities. A large number of these young boys have no caring adult in their lives, no father or male mentor who will provide adult leadership. So young boys turn to gangs to give them a sense of safety and belonging.

Many mothers have talked to me about their feelings of inadequacy in parenting their sons. I stress to them that boys need to see their moms as a serious form of structure. If you are unsure of yourself, your son will sense that and walk all over you. Boys act tough to cover up their own fears and inadequacies. If you will step up and clearly establish yourself as the boss, they relax. Boys need clear and consistent discipline. You have to look them in the eye and lay down the law.

One summer I worked as a lifeguard for a public pool in my hometown. Many parents would allow their older children to spend much of the day at the pool, unsupervised. For weeks I had been dealing with a handful of ten-year-old boys who thought they owned the pool. I had told them time and time again that I was going to throw them out if they didn't straighten up, but since I never followed through with my actions they never believed me. I liked them, they were good boys, but they were getting out of control.

Finally, about halfway through the summer, I followed through. I blew the whistle, emptied the pool, and walked all five of them to the front gate. I told them if their parents had any questions they could call me. I will never forget the shocked looked on their faces as they dejectedly walked away.

The next day the boys showed up at the pool right as we opened the gate. The guy taking the money at the front gate refused to let them in until I approved it. I stared at them and looked as if I was debating long and hard. Finally I agreed, but I told them that the first time they didn't listen they were out. Amazingly, the five little devils suddenly became sweet boys again. The rest of the summer I had no problems from them.

I learned an important lesson that day: you can be kind and fair and still be strict. Boys need to know where the line is, and they need to know that you are serious when they cross it.

Chemically boys are also very different. Boys' brains make less of certain chemicals like serotonin. This makes it harder for them to sit still and focus on what someone is saying to them. Because of these differences boys respond better to symbols and pictures, and they tend to learn higher math and physics better than girls. This is part of the reason that video games are so appealing to boys. They enjoy moving characters around and controlling their movements.

Testosterone is the male hormone that also plays a significant part in the development of a boy. An increase in the levels of testosterone will start around puberty and cause a deeper voice, bigger muscles, and facial and body hair. The hormone may also cause restlessness, disorganization, and forgetfulness. Your son will probably go through mood swings where he is argumentative about everything. And of course, it will be easy during this time for him to act first and think later. Do your homework and be prepared for the changes your son will be experiencing. Your sensitivity will pay off in your relationship with your son.

Of course boys' hormones don't tell the whole story. Each boy has his own temperament, family background, and environment that can also make a difference in how he develops. As you think about your own sons, think about their ages, their personalities, and the fact that being a guy is really different than being a girl. It's easy for moms to try to reach their boys from their own set of female references. In most cases this will not work. In order to help them learn important life lessons, you must find the way they learn best. Study your boys. Take time to learn about how they are different, and then work out a plan to make sure they are gaining the morals and character that would honor the Lord and your family name.

Boys and Their Moms

Mothers do so many things like no one else; this is why we need them so much. Mothers can comfort and support in a special way that works magic on the soul. Boys need their mothers to help teach them about love and trust in a way that will help them become stronger men. Many times mothers feel they need to push their sons away so they can become masculine. Nothing could be further from the truth. The connection that mothers establish with their sons will actually play an important part in developing masculinity.

In researching for this book I was overwhelmed at the number of negative statistics regarding boys. It wouldn't take long to begin to feel that boys are inferior and have little chance of turning out to be great men. Nothing could be further from the truth. I am afraid in people's attempts to prove that girls are just as good as boys they have skewed the data to imply that boys are not as good as girls.

God has used men throughout the ages to lead the world in a way that only they can. He has gifted them and designed them, not as inferior but as capable and perfect for the job He has called them to do. As a teacher, I enjoyed having young men in my classes. Their discussions were always open and honest. They had a wonderful ability to see through the clutter and go directly to the point.

Growing up with two brothers taught me early that boys have no tolerance for "the long version" or "the whiney version." On many occasions my brothers' words of wisdom have been "just get over it and move on." It was hard to swallow at first. I didn't want to get over it, I wanted to wallow in certain situations and have them feel sorry for me. Soon I realized that it wasn't going to happen and I took their advice. It has proved to be the best decision on many occasions since.

Males have wonderful strengths and abilities that women do not. Women need men to be the hero, to protect them, to defend them, and to help them navigate life. We need their different perspectives to balance our world and for them to walk in front of us, leading the way. This may not be the politically correct jargon of our day, but if boys are going to be the men that they were designed by God to be, then they must understand their role.

Boys need their mothers to help them define these roles. Today our culture has blended the sexes into a gender-blind movement where the difference between the sexes is obsolete. Mothers can counteract that by helping their sons become true men. Truett Cathey, the founder of Chick-fil-A, once said, "I would rather build boys than mend men." His point is so true; it is better for us to start while they are young and teach boys what it is to be a man than try to take men and teach them how to grow up and overcome their adolescence.

Although their dads will play a crucial role in this process of a boy's life, mothers also have a part to play. Dads will cast a vision for their sons, help them define their lives, teach them to accept the responsibility that God has given them, and set a model for them to follow. Mothers help their sons understand and know how to treat the opposite sex. Mothers help their sons establish a good self-image. Mothers also teach their sons how to do the practical things in life.

I think one of the greatest gifts a mother can give her son is the ability to be friends with a woman. Through the years I have watched young men and women try to socialize in the college setting. Young men who had learned how to cultivate a friendship with young women seemed more self-confident, were more focused on their responsibilities, and ended up with the best girls. Young men who learn to develop friendships learn to communicate with girls in a relaxed and comfortable way. They learn to establish physical boundaries that protect both the girl and themselves. As friends, they learn to listen to the hearts of the girls they meet. Listening to the heart of a friend teaches them so much about what kind of girl they want to marry and spend the rest of their lives with.

One of the things I respect so much about my mother and father's relationship was their willingness to share in the work. My brothers learned how to do laundry, how to cook, how to iron their shirts, and how to clean the house. My dad was not afraid he would appear less masculine if he ran the vacuum cleaner or did a load of laundry. Guys need to learn these basic skills because many of them will live on their own before they get married, and they will need to know how to function without Mom around. In addition, when they do get married, their wives will appreciate the fact that they have married a team player. Young men need to understand that women are not their slaves. They need to be taught that real men help their wives with whatever task is needed. I admire both of my brothers greatly. It is not unusual to walk into their homes and find them ironing their kids' clothes or cooking supper. They have grown up to be men with wonderful hearts for their wives and children.

Another important part of a boy's education regarding girls is that not all girls are nice. Proverbs talks about an evil woman who lurks about trying to seduce young men and lure them into sin. From Bible times until present day these women still exist. The concern is that they are becoming so aggressive so young. Boys need to learn how to spot a girl who is aggressive and up to no good. He needs to learn how to navigate out of harm's way before he can't think clearly. As a mom, you can help him in this area by teaching what to look for and how to respond.

A mom is the best cheerleader her child can have. As children grow up they need to be encouraged and filled with positive affirmation. Boys learn a lot about the world around them when someone helps them see it. Take the time to point out the beauty of a sunset or the cuteness of a puppy, and he will learn to appreciate the world around him. Tell him how good he looks when he dresses up a bit or puts on a new outfit. This will remind him that how he dresses is important and clean clothes are noticed.

Boys can be very affectionate and tender, and this side of them needs to be affirmed. Help him feel safe and secure when he is vulnerable or shares a deep hurt with you. Let him know that it's good to share his feelings with other people he trusts. Share in his interests and encourage him to be balanced with his activities. Go to his ballgames, get him a library card, and go there with him. Let him know that you care about what is interesting to him.

My friend Margaret has a twelve-year-old son named Zach who has loved animals since he was just a little guy. He likes bugs, fish, and quite a few other interesting animals. Margaret is not exactly what you would call a scaredy-cat, but she is not one who would voluntarily have bugs in her home either. However, Zach likes these animals, so he has had an ant farm, a crab, a praying mantis, a gecko, and numerous fish.

Not long ago I spent the day with Margaret and her family at the two aquariums in Chattanooga. It was a fun time for all of us, but Zach truly had a blast. He knew a whole lot of information about many of the fish we saw that day. I thought about Zach as I stood watching two divers enter the tanks and swim among the fish. One day he will probably be doing something just like that because he has a mother who supports and encourages his interests.

Young Men That Rise Above

In 1 Timothy 4, Paul instructs Timothy in his responsibilities as a young man entrusted with leading others in the way of Christ. In the midst of a long list of instructions, Paul reinforces Timothy's ability to do the job God has called him to: "Let no man despise thy youth; but be thou an example of the believers, in word, in conversation, in charity, in spirit, in faith, in purity" (verse 12). If young men are going to rise above the status quo and do something for God, they are going to have to hold these words close to their hearts.

It starts by being an example. Your actions will always speak louder than your words. Teach your sons to start their quest for manhood and responsibility by taking responsibility for their own actions. Help them to understand the vital importance of leading by example so that no one can think little of them because they are young. Paul gives Timothy a list of areas he needed to focus on. As his parent, I think it is important for you to challenge your son with the following list as well.

Word—This is his speech. Teach him the importance of guarding his tongue and choosing his words wisely. Learning to think before we speak is a vital lesson for all of us.

Conversation—This is his conduct. Teach him that his behavior and manner of life really matter. Remind him that he has two family names to protect: yours and the name of Christ. If he wants more freedom, he must show that he values his testimony and makes good decisions.

Charity—This is his ability to show love. Teach him that real men show compassion and love to others. He needs to learn to protect those who are weaker than him and to exhibit a heart full of good will to others. Jesus was such a wonderful example of a powerful man who loved greatly. He was open with His words of love and affection to everyone around Him. For your son, his greatest test will come at home as he demonstrates this love to his family.

Spirit—This is his spiritual-mindedness. Teach your son to cultivate a meaningful personal relationship with Jesus Christ. As he matures he should not have to rely on his parents or the church alone to give him spiritual meat. As he reads God's Word and prays, God will begin to speak to him personally and show him his purpose in life.

Faith—This word indicates two concepts that blend together to help your son build a strong foundation to stand on. First is the concept of truth. A person's faith is founded in what he believes to be true, or his convictions. This relates to his faith in God the creator, Jesus the redeemer, and the Holy Spirit, the counselor. Your son must develop his own convictions about his beliefs. Once he does this, he must stand on those by faith and trust in God to be true to His Word.

The second aspect of this word is faithfulness or fidelity. It's the idea that your son can be relied on to be faithful to his word. Young men must understand their word to someone is valuable. Commitment is hard to find in today's young people. They would rather keep every option open until the last minute. But part of his transition into manhood is leaving childish things behind. A man's word should be his bond.

Purity—This is his dedication to live a holy life. Purity is more than just a word that deals with sexual activities. It encompasses a person's whole lifestyle. We cannot achieve this in our own strength no matter how hard we try. But Christ works in us and through us to give us the ability to be holy. Teach your son the importance of allowing Christ to make his life holy by surrendering his will and his ways to God. Encourage him to walk in obedience, to flee from temptation, and to arm himself with the whole armor of God so that he can resist the devil. His dedication to a pure life will bring great blessings into his life now and in the days to come.

Paul tells Timothy that if he will do these things, he will save himself and those around him whom he influences with his life and his words. I cannot think of a greater challenge for our young men than the ones laid down in this passage. We need young men who will rise above mediocrity and take up the challenge to dare for more from themselves.

Society may not expect much, but as a parent, you must give them a vision of a man who through a relationship with Christ rises above what others expect. Alone he can do nothing, but through Christ all things are possible. I believe with all my heart that God is searching across the face of the globe for young men who will step up and surrender their lives to His call. As God equips them, He will send them out to make a difference in every city, in every marketplace, in every field, and in every home.

When you expect greatness from someone, you set the stage for him to be great. Suddenly he sees the world from a different perspective; he begins to believe that maybe, just maybe, it's possible. As his thinking is stretched, he begins to set his goals higher. It takes courage to expect greatness from your children, but I don't think that anything less should be in your thoughts. They don't have to be a straight-A student to be great. They don't have to be the leading scorer on the team to be great. In fact, they don't have to be gifted in any area to achieve greatness. Remember, God is not looking for those who have it all together and always do it well. He is looking for those who will surrender their average, below average, normal, not-so-normal, messed-up, sin-stained lives to Him, and let Him get all the glory for doing the miraculous through the simple.

One boy had only a few fish and a couple pieces of bread (John 6:1–14). I am sure he was shocked to find that Christ wanted them. But then an amazing thing happened. Christ took his simple lunch, blessed it, and fed thousands. I would have loved to have seen his mother's face when he came home to tell her the story. Or maybe she was there, beaming with pride as she watched her son's small sacrifice touch so many lives.

Oh, how blessed our children would be if they could see the unlimited vastness of God's touch on a person's life. "The world has yet to see what God can do with and for and through and in and by the man who is fully and wholly consecrated to Him." Dwight L. Moody was challenged one day by this simple statement uttered by Henry Varley, a British revivalist. Moody was so moved by what Varley had said that a year later he returned to England and told him about how God had used those words in his life. According to the story, Henry Varley could not even remember what he had said to Moody that day. But it would be a declaration that would forever impact Moody's life. In fact, this quotation has become so associated with Moody that many do not know that it did not originate with him. He did, however, add his own ending: "I will try my utmost to be that man."[27]

I pray that you sense the urgency to expect greatness from your teens and young adults. Encourage your boys and girls alike to set the bar high and then reach for it. Don't give up on them! Continue to lay the next step before them, and pray and cheer and believe until they take it.

Chapter 14

Brains and Brawn

Winning the Sex War

The military understands the importance of educating the troops and takes an active role in making sure all military personnel have opportunities to further their education both while they are in the service and after they get out. They realize that it takes more than just tough soldiers to win battles—they also have to be smart. From the military academies to the G.I. Bill, soldiers have opportunities to get a great education that will carry them from the battlefield to a career.

If our children are going to be battle ready they also have to be strong and smart. One of the greatest battles they will ever fight will be the sex war. It is important that we do more than just tell them to be strong and say "no." Sex education is a necessary step in making sure they can outthink and outsmart the enemy. I am convinced that one of the keys to fighting the sex war is for parents to become the leading authority on sex for their children. As godly parents educate their children about sexual issues, they can give them a clearly defined sense of morality and both the brawn and the brains to follow God's plan for their lives.

Start Young

Most children begin to realize the differences between the sexes at around two years of age. They may ask unusual questions during these earlier years, but they are usually not for sexually related reasons. Questions such as "Mommy, why is he different than me?" "Where do babies come from?" Even though these questions are innocent, your reaction as a mother is extremely important. They will learn what is acceptable and unacceptable to discuss as they watch your reaction. They also will also begin a very important process of communication with you that will last throughout their lives. Understanding at a very early age that they can talk with you about any topic is an important building block to future communication.

Teaching them the principles of appropriateness and privacy is also important as they mature. I encourage parents to use the correct biological terminology when teaching their children about their bodies and how they work. I think this helps take the embarrassment out of using certain words such as *penis* or *vagina*. I also think this begins to build a platform for parents to pursue more mature conversations. As your children get older, you will need to discuss many sensitive areas. Using the correct terminology brings science and biology into play as serious subject matters and avoids the silliness of childish terms that don't seem to fit the nature of the discussion.

Another reason I think correct terminology is important is so that there is no confusion. The world has many slang terms for sex and for a person's body parts. Slang tends to make the topic crude or vulgar. It also tends to make it funny for young people who are already embarrassed by the topic and need something to hide behind. Teach children that slang, in this area, is not appropriate.

Don't Wait Till It's Too Late

I was working at a camp one summer as a lifeguard and camp counselor when a young eleven-year-old girl came up to me in tears. Seeing that she was very hesitant to tell me what was wrong, I took her off to the side and begged her to tell me. Finally through sobs she muttered, "I cut my backside."

Unsure I had heard her correctly, I repeated it. "You cut your backside?"

She nodded.

"How did you do that?" I asked.

With tears streaming down her face and a look of fear in her eyes, she muttered, "I don't know, all I know is that I am bleeding down there."

In the next few moments I realized what was happening and reassured the girl that she was going to be fine. The camp director's wife sat down with this young girl and introduced her to the facts of life.

At the time I thought this story was quite humorous. Now I see it as a sad picture of how one mother failed to guide her daughter through the first stretch of very difficult times. Starting your period for the first time can be traumatic enough for many young girls. Starting it away from home is another blow, but not understanding what is happening to you and thinking you are seriously hurt or dying is quite another thing altogether. I am sure her mother had many reasons why she had failed to talk with her daughter, but she missed an important opportunity to invest in her future.

Many mothers don't talk to their children about issues such as puberty, menstrual cycles, sex, and other related issues because their mothers didn't talk to them. Since they seem to have made it without too much damage, they figure their kids will too. Other mothers tried to talk with their daughters but were met with opposition so they gave up. Still others wait, thinking their child is too young to be told yet, and are blindsided when she develops faster than they expected.

Obviously this is not an easy issue to discuss with your "baby." But please understand it is not easy to discuss with your "mother" either. This is why it is so important to start opening up the lines of communication at an early age. I hope that by the time "the talk" is necessary, the openness you have established with your children will pay off.

Take the Mystery Out of Sex

Sex is not a dirty word and is not a topic that should be avoided. The world uses it to sell everything from toothpaste to cell phones. Musical artists sing about it, actors romanticize it, so parents have to *normalize* it. What does that mean? Normalize simply means to make something normal—to take the mystery out of it.

When I was the dean of women at a Christian university, I would often try to warn parents when I saw their daughter self-destructing. Although I don't remember many of those conversations, one will forever stick out in my mind. I called a mother one day to talk to her about her freshman daughter. Sally was pushing the limits in every area, racking up demerits for almost every violation in the student handbook. She was doing poorly in many of her classes, and she had been caught in precarious situations with guys on several occasions; at this point she was headed for real trouble. I tried almost every angle to help, but she refused to listen.

I called her mom for help and support from home. After explaining to her mom the variety of trouble we were having with Sally, I asked her if she had experienced these same problems at home. I will never forget the shrill but defensive tone of her voice as she replied, "Our Sally is not allowed to date or even be alone with a boy at any time. She would never do the things you have mentioned unless some boy was forcing her. I will have you know, Miss Bowman, that the 'S' word is never used in our home, so it is not my daughter with the problem."

Although I am sure this dear mother had the best intentions for her daughter, she had done her a large disservice. The "mystery" of all these feelings and changes, which by the way are God-given, had heightened the level of sexual curiosity in this girl. Now she was determined to find out what all the fuss was about. Remember, what you don't say often speaks louder than what you do say. If your children don't get clear biblical teaching from you, they will get an education from other sources. Unfortunately many teenagers and young adults, like Sally, get their education in the back seat of a car. By the time they figure out that this is not the fairy-tale they thought it was, many of them have lost their purity or become pregnant, as

Sally did only a few short months after the conversation I had with her mom.

God created our bodies and He created sex. Sex is not dirty unless it is perverted or taken out of the confines of God's commands. Parents can help take the mystery out of puberty and sex one piece at a time. Young people need to understand that God created men and women differently. They need to know how they are different. Keeping these conversations simple will help you know how much information your child needs at each point and in what format to give it to them. Correct terminology helps keep things simple.

As they grow older and begin to ask more questions, treat those questions seriously. If you avoid the questions or have a complete meltdown because of what your child has just said, the questions will quickly end. You will teach them that you cannot handle this type of conversation and they will go somewhere else for answers.

Teens need to know they can talk about puberty, sex, and all that those issues entail with their parents. Most parents want their teens to talk to them about anything, but when the time really comes they don't know how to handle it. Early preparation is key.

I can remember when I was training to be a lifeguard there were certain maneuvers they taught us to do in the shallow end first. We would practice until we had a good feel for what we were to do, then we would move out to the deep end. I think the same principle applies when working up to these key areas of conversations with children. Start when they are young, and as you move to deeper water both of you will be better prepared to handle the topic.

Teachable Moments

One mother told me the story of how she overheard her nine-year-old telling her school friend that if you kissed a boy for more than five seconds you would get pregnant. At first she was elated, thinking, *Great, she won't be kissing any boys anytime soon.* Then she realized several things. First, this information was incorrect. Second, her nine-year-old daughter was talking about kissing and having babies! Red flags began to go up as she recalled her daughter's conversation.

Later that night while cleaning up after supper she asked her daughter what she thought about kissing boys. At first she was shy and reluctant to say anything. But as she saw her mother's smile and heard the pleasantness in her voice, she began to laugh. As the dishes were washed and the table was cleared, this mom was able to get her daughter to talk about kissing. By the time the floor was swept, this mom had not only dealt with the incorrect information, but she had helped her daughter begin to deal with the issue of physical relationships. She allowed her daughter to guide the conversation and she never laughed at her misguided ideas. They didn't discuss sex that night because her daughter wasn't ready, but her mother told her that anytime she wanted to ask a question or to verify something she had heard at school that she could come to her and it would be their secret. Several months later over another set of dirty dishes she talked to her daughter about her period and not long after that about sex.

Several things about that mother's story make it positive. First of all, doing other things while talking made the conversation easier. Children are different and some of them really respond to sitting down across from each other, eyeball to eyeball. But for most preteens this situation is one they want to avoid at all cost, because the intensity makes them uncomfortable and apprehensive. Not to mention, what it does to the parent who is trying to figure out what to say and how much to say.

Second, because the mother was listening she hit upon a topic that was relevant and something she knew her daughter was thinking about. It also gave her a starting point for the conversation. A teachable moment is priceless and doesn't come around very often of its own accord; you must keep your ears open and create an environment that fosters these moments.

Initiate Conversations

Although you should be alert for teachable moments, you don't necessarily have to wait for one. One of the greatest myths I find among mothers is that they assume the young person should initiate all conversations of this nature. Nothing could be further from the truth. As a general rule your teenager is not going to come to you and initiate conversations regarding these types of topics. Most of the time, *you* will need to initiate the conversation. Not only will you need to give the basic biological information, but you will also need to be very clear about your stance on the moral and spiritual aspects of sex. The blanket "don't have sex before marriage" message does not suffice anymore.

Bill Albert, the communications director for the National Campaign to Prevent Teen Pregnancy, urges parents to be more specific when they talk to their children about sex. Based on a report released by the National Center for Health in 2005, over half of all teenagers ages fifteen to nineteen have engaged in oral sex. Albert comments, "We used to talk about sex in terms of first base, second base, and so on. Oral sex was maybe in the dugout. If [parents] want their teens to abstain from sex, they need to say exactly what they want their kids to abstain from."[28] It is not enough to present the short list of do's and don'ts to young people and expect them to generalize. Parents must be specific.

Many teens consider themselves "technical virgins" because they have not had intercourse. Teens don't consider "hooking up" or "friends with benefits" to be an issue from a moral perspective. Most teenagers who have had oral sex think of themselves as virgins. Are these the values you want your children to have? If not, you need to spell out clearly God's teachings about sex. And that means talking to your child in sometimes uncomfortable detail.

Several years ago a movie called *American Pie* came out. The target audience was teenagers; the theme was teenagers and sex. The message was simple: teenagers look at pornography; teenagers masturbate; teenagers are not required to love someone to have sex—if you like them, it's okay to sleep with them. In fact, according to this movie, if you don't have sex at the prom you are the biggest idiot alive. The movie glamorized sex and being "used" for sex. Where were the parents, you ask? Well, the goofy, stupid parents didn't have a clue what was going on. The message was clear—parents are old, uninformed, and don't understand the feelings teenagers face. The values that parents have make them archaic and stupid.

So aren't there a few movies out there that teach moral values and the concept of right and wrong? Mel Gibson, in the movie *What*

Women Want, was applauded for dealing with the issue of sexually active teenagers. But let's take a closer look before we start clapping. His character is a divorced father who is very sexually promiscuous personally, but when he finds out that his daughter is planning to have sex, he comes unglued. But being the good guy that he is, he finds time to talk to his daughter about sex, and his advice is simple: "You should love someone very much before you have sex." In the end his daughter chooses not to have sex because she doesn't love the guy, and we applaud. But what message has been sent? What values have been taught? Moral values and the importance of right and wrong are not discussed in this movie. Today, you have high morals if you don't have sex until you're older and truly love someone and if you practice "safe sex" when you are ready to become active.

Is that the message you want your children to believe? If not, you had better start talking and combating the message, because that is the message they are getting. Sex cannot be discussed without biblical truth, or you only have information with no value system. From an early age children understand the difference between right and wrong. As they hit their preteen years they begin to realize that lightning will not strike them if they question the reasons behind those absolutes. At this time parents should be ready to deal with questions and situations that might strike against the values they have tried to instill in their child.

Many times your children are not *rebelling* against your values, they are *processing* them. As a child grows physically they also grow mentally. The older they become, the more they are able to manage abstract concepts, such as, "Mom, if it is okay to disagree with the preacher on this point, then why can't I disagree with him on this one too?" Granted these questions keep us on our toes and are not easy to answer, but if we don't "freak out" and commit to work through these issues with our children, then they will continue to ask us the hard questions. More important, they will feel they are free to ask controversial questions knowing that their parents will not think they are bad or on their way to hell. Which, believe it or not, is the second most popular reason that I was given as to why teenagers felt they couldn't talk to their parents.

Friendship with the Opposite Sex

As the barriers between the sexes have been torn down, boys and girls are increasingly more comfortable having friendships with someone of the opposite sex. However, the lines of friendship sometimes can be blurred as a result of the "friends with benefits" concept, in which teens engage in physical activity with a casual acquaintance or even a good friend. Kissing, making out (clothes on but touching on top of clothes), and heavy petting (hand under clothes or clothes coming off) are not considered a big deal among teens today. Sadly, teens involved in this type of behavior have no concept of true friendship with the opposite sex.

Some parents who hear of this trend may want to ban opposite-sex friendships altogether. That is not the answer. Teens need to learn to build strong friendships. This will fill the need they have for socialization and help them learn what they are looking for in a future mate, as they get to know different personalities, practice communication, and explore mutual interests. Stressing friendship over getting serious or having a steady date is so much better for them during their teen years.

Dating, Courtship, or Whatever You Want to Call It

This brings me to the subject of dating. There are many different philosophies about dating. I am not here to debate those or to argue for one position. My concern is not how young people go about meeting each other and choosing a life's mate, but the fact that they do. Healthy young people should have friends of both sexes. Whether at church or at school, they interact with their friends on a daily basis. As they grow older and begin to be interested in each other physically and emotionally, their relationships are elevated. My question is, are their morals and standards elevated in preparation for this interaction? These days teens do not have to go on an official date to be in a relationship. In fact, as I already mentioned, they do not even have to like each other to be physically involved! If you are going to expect more from your teenager, then you must prepare her in the area of relationships.

Regardless of your position on teen dating, you must prepare your young person to interact with the opposite sex. This involves friendship, hanging out, physical boundaries, emotional attachments, and so much more. Have you talked to her about these areas? Have you helped to guide her to the higher ground?

The world's philosophy is easily identified. You don't have to listen long to hear it coming from every portal. Nike says, "Just do it." Sprite encourages you to "Obey your thirst." Popular teen shows encourage young people to do what feels good. Pleasure is the determining factor for so many people's moral choices. Young people must rise above this way of thinking or they will spend their lives sacrificing the permanent on the altar of the immediate.

When pleasure is the determining factor, attraction to the opposite sex is a field of land mines. Our young people must understand that this "feel-good" approach is not the best choice. Here is an opportunity to elevate. God designed physical touch to feel good. He wired our bodies so that we would derive pleasure from kissing and making out. One of the worst tactics you can take is to try to convince your teen that they won't like it. Sure they will, at least we hope so! They are normal if their heart races and they want to make out with the person to whom they are attracted.

God has their best in mind. He knows that they will find the ultimate fulfillment of the physical relationship in marriage. Scripture is so elevated in its call for our lives. It calls us to live a sacrificial life. The biblical life is a life that sacrifices temporary pleasure with pain in the end, for temporary restraint with pleasure in the end. It's a good trade. Sure, it's hard to keep your emotions in check and say "no" to temptation. That is why young people need to understand the importance of setting parameters in their social lives.

What Are Your Dating Standards?

Over the years I have asked thousands of teenagers these two questions:

1. Do you have any dating/social standards?
2. If so, what are they?

Although I never did the actual statistics (I wish I had now), I can safely say that more than 75 percent of them said yes to question #1. Out of that group, the majority had the same basic answer to question #2. The standards were simple: they would only date people who are Christians, and they were not going to have sex until they got married.

Sounds good, doesn't it? Sadly, moms, it's not enough.

I have talked to hundreds of girls who sat with purity rings on their fingers and told me they were having sex with their boyfriends. Oh, they never intended to go that far. It started simple enough, but quickly got out of control. They always thought they could control it, but they couldn't. You see, that is the problem; we were never designed to control it. There is not an on/off switch on our hormones that we can control like a light bulb. God designed one physical action to lead to another one as a process of preparing the body for sexual intercourse. He never intended that we spend our teen years trying to stop right before we hit the point of no return.

If teens are going keep their purity they must elevate and increase their barriers of protection. Help your young people by sitting them down and discussing these vital areas of importance. Notice I said "discussing" and not mandating. This approach will really help as you determine where your young person already stands and what temptations she is dealing with. It doesn't matter what approach to dating you take; this conversation is necessary. If you have teens that go outside of the house, they will interact with the opposite sex. Remember, your goal is not to box your children in, but to prepare them to live in the world. You will probably have many conversations along this line as your teenager strives to stay pure.

Young people need to make up their mind about how they are going to behave before they enter into social settings. If they are allowed to date, whether single or double dating, they need to think about where they should and shouldn't go on their dates. They need to understand why secluded areas like bedrooms and basements are not best for staying pure. I am floored at the number of parents who allow their young person and their boyfriends and girlfriends to hang out unsupervised in their homes. A house full of beds and comfortable furniture is a temptation that should be guarded against.

Insist on Modesty

Today the theme for our girls is sexy. Everything circles around being sexy and dressing sexy. Girls are indoctrinated at an early age that you have to have a boyfriend to be popular and the way to get a boyfriend is to be provocative. It is difficult to insist on modesty in this atmosphere but not impossible. We must remember that God is still on the throne and His message is still the same. First Timothy 2:9 tells women to dress in modest apparel, which is clothing that is clean and decent, but not over the top. Dressing modestly is dressing in a way that does not draw undue attention to your body.

Over and over again Scripture speaks of lust and the importance of guarding against it. Men are cautioned about looking at women and lusting after them and women are cautioned about acting in ways that cause men to stumble. Modesty is more than just how your daughter dresses; it's an issue of the heart. It must start with a conscious decision to "possess [her] vessel in sanctification and honour" (1 Thessalonians 4:4). It's about asking yourself what would honor God and what would show honor to those around you. It's surrendering your desire to be popular and stylish over being holy.

Modesty is not just a topic for "girls only." Although guys approach dress in a different way than girls, they also should realize that modesty is important. Boys need to understand that their dress communicates a lot about who they are and what they are about. Their heart is revealed through their actions and attitudes. A teen boy who is taught to be modest in his speech and his conduct will be on his way to becoming like Christ in his life.

> I beseech you therefore brethren, by the mercies of God, that you present your bodies a living sacrifice, holy, acceptable unto God, which is your reasonable service. And be not conformed to this world; but be ye transformed by the renewing of your mind they you may prove what is that good and acceptable, and perfect will of God. (Romans 12:1–2)

As girls transform into young women, they must be taught how their dress affects young men. Dress is an important part of social interaction. How a person dresses affects her reputation and the attention she gets from the opposite sex. Our girls need to know that sex may sell, but when they dress in a sexy way it comes across as if *they* are for sale. A girl cheapens her value and chips away at her self-worth when she dresses as an object and not a person.

As girls raise the level of their dress from sexy and provocative to modest and stylish, they immediately send out a signal that they are not "that kind of girl." The guys who are hanging around for what they can get physically will hang out somewhere else. The best part is that good young men who are looking for girls who want to stay pure and holy in their relationships will know that this girl is worth getting to know.

Gray Rape and Date Rape

Rape is a hard thing to think about much less talk to your children about. However, for the sake of our children's safety it is necessary. Part of teaching our children to be smart and strong is teaching them to say "no" soon enough and forceful enough. I encourage you to teach your children to stand their ground and say "no." Don't assume your children will never be placed in an uncomfortable situation with the opposite sex—assume they will. Prepare both your sons and daughters for aggressive people.

It used to be that boys chased and girls ran. Today that is not the case. In many cases girls have turned into the pursuers. Young men need to know how to avoid these types of girls and how to get out of awkward situations with poise.

Aggressive guys can physically and mentally overpower girls. Girls need to be taught how to avoid situations that could be potentially hazardous and how to fight back both verbally and physically.

In the new hook-up culture, kids start messing around and then don't want to stop. When one of them realizes they have gone much farther than they intended and tries to shut things down, it can often be difficult. A new term has emerged for this kind of date rape; they call it "gray rape." This is where one of the people involved didn't want it to go that far and had difficulty communicating that fact or had difficulty stopping the aggressor. The reason it's called "gray" is because a girl feels she carries some responsibility for what happened even though she wanted it to stop.

In the majority of cases, drugs and alcohol play a large role in date rape. Drinking dulls the senses and loosens inhibitions. Parents need to warn their kids against drinking and expect them to act responsibly.

There are many things you can do to help your children protect themselves. Teach them to avoid spending time with someone who makes them feel uneasy or uncomfortable. Girls need to learn to follow their instincts when that little voice is telling them this guy is bad news. Teach them to stay away from drugs and alcohol. Encourage them to go out with a group of friends, especially if they are just getting to know a new person. Make sure they understand that they should never meet someone in person that they have only met over the Internet or by phone.

Teach your children to call for help when they need it. Many girls I have talked with are afraid to call their parents because they are more afraid of their parent's reaction than they are of getting hurt. This is crazy. You must assure your daughter that if she gets uncomfortable she should call you and you will help her without overreacting. You can discuss her poor decisions or her disobedience after you have her safe and at home. When she calls you, don't fuss or shout—just make sure you get her in a safe situation as soon as possible.

Last but not least, I think that every girl should take a self-defense class. As a general rule boys are stronger and more adept at defending themselves from girls, but girls tend to be the weaker one in most social situations and it will help them to know how to respond if they ever feel threatened. I encourage moms to take the course as well. It will be a fun thing to do with your daughter and it will give you both some needed skills and confidence.

Elevate Moral Standards

Swimming upstream is not easy, especially when you are a teenager. The desire is so strong to be popular and liked by the peer group that many times young people do things that they know are not right just to fit in. It seems they can't understand the seriousness of their choices. When you are young it's easy to think you will live forever and that every thing is "fixable." Unfortunately this is not true. Although God is gracious and He forgives much, there are still scars that people carry throughout this life as a result of the sins of their youth. As a mother, I know you want to help your young person avoid these scars. I know it is possible.

Over the past twenty years I have met some great young people. They are scattered all over the globe today doing amazing things for God. Some are in a ministry, some are stay-at-home moms, some are influencing their career area, but each of them is making an impact for God in the world.

What is the cause of their success? It's not their talent level or their people skills. It cannot be attributed to their personality, background, or upbringing. It is not based on where they went to school or what type of church they attend. When I think of them I find that they have one common attribute: they are living above the expectation level. They demanded more from themselves. They set their standard higher and pushed for more.

These young people elevated their moral standards in spite of the crowd, without concern for their popularity. They learned that if they were going to make their decisions based on the crowd they would always be in chaos. Somewhere along the way they found the strength to swim upstream, and that decision has forever affected their lives. Robert Frost said it well, "Two roads diverged in a wood, and I—I took the one less traveled by, and that has made all the difference."

Part Four

My Mama Is the Real Deal

Chapter 15

Like an Arrow

Launching Your Young Adult

One of the first weapons used in warfare by all civilizations was the bow and arrow, which took great skill and precision to use. Whether trying to shoot an animal for your next meal or take down an enemy, you had to take into consideration many factors: the distance of the shot, the movement of the target, the direction of the wind, and much more. Shooting an arrow to hit its target was a skill that took great precision and patience.

Many parents feel a sense of helplessness when it comes time for their children to leave home and start life on their own. But I don't think this is the feeling that you should have at all. Since the day they came into this world you have been preparing them to stand on their own two feet and make an impact on the world around them. You have prayed for them, cried with them, and encouraged them to grow in every area of their lives. With patience and precision you have considered every possible factor, and now is the moment to release them as a master archer releases an arrow, trusting it to hit its target.

Straight-Flying Arrows

We can learn much about releasing our bow with confidence from King David. In Psalm 127, David uses the visual image of an arrow to represent a child.

Like arrows in the hand of a warrior, So are the children of one's youth. How blessed is the man whose quiver is full of them. (Psalm 127:4–5a NASB)

David was a man who would appreciate a good bow and arrow. He had spent much of his life perfecting his skills in the use of such a weapon. He knew how important it was to have an arrow that would fly straight. I am sure that while protecting sheep or defending himself from Saul and his enemies he had depended on straight-flying arrows to kill his supper and protect him from danger.

In David's day, men made their own arrows. Each one had to be made correctly so it would do the job. The shaft had to be made of the correct wood, the feathers had to be positioned just right, the tip had to be sharp and weighted properly. Each detail of the arrow was important. Then you were blessed if you had a bunch of them in your pack.

David reminds us that children are like arrows. As a parent it is your job to make sure they are ready to fly, then at the appropriate time they will serve as a strength and a defense for your family as they are launched and find their target. It's a beautiful picture of the process of preparation and presentation. Releasing a young person that you have had a part in crafting, and watching them accelerate to their God-given target is a gratifying and rich reward for any parent. God says this is your heritage and His gift to you.

Let Them Fly!

The transition from high school to college and career can be an exciting and stressful time. For parents the fear of letting their children leave home and go out on their own can be daunting. Mothers especially want to hold on to their baby just a little while longer. Your instinct will be to maintain control and keep the reins held tight. Parents use guilt, bribery, threats, and even intimidation to keep their young people from stepping out on their own. You may win the battle, but your child will lose in the long run. Your young adult needs his freedom if he is going to go on to the next level.

One of my jobs as dean of women was to help run freshman orientation. During this time we conducted several informative sessions for parents of new students. My session with the parents was always the last one, held on the day many of them would be leaving their children behind and heading home. The session was on letting go. I was always moved as I watched parents wiping away tears as I spoke.

I encouraged these parents to go home and pray for their kids. I told them what to expect from their newly acquired college freshman, how they would come home at Christmas break different. It was a hard transition time for everyone, but they would make it. And last, I warned them of the dangers of refusing to let go. There are only two outcomes when they refuse to let go, and neither of them are good ones. Either their child would submit to their authority and never grow, or they would rebel, and anger and resentment would enter the relationship.

Young adult children still need you, but not in the same way they needed you in the past. They now need your friendship and advice. Yes, you have spent twenty or more years loving them and taking care of their every need, and it's hard to let go, but you must. Young adults still have many dangerous decisions to make, and they need the guidance and support of their families. During their early twenties most of them will make career decisions, marital decisions, and financial decisions. They need to make these decisions by seeking the will of God for their lives, by surrendering to God's will, and by focusing on the future God has for them. They will need your encouragement to do this.

I was asked one time why I taught my college classes with such passion. For me the answer was simple; in just four short years these students would graduate and leave. My class, and others just like it, was the last time many of these students would be taught in the classroom. Once you graduate, life teaches you by experience, and the school of hard knocks is a tough one. For four years I had an opportunity to impact them, to help them learn the easy way, to remind them of what was important, and hopefully to reinforce what their parents had spent their lifetime trying to teach. Once their tassels are moved and their caps tossed much of their accountability is gone. It's all up to them now.

I was never more aware of this fact than the day I stood and watched Brandi toss her own cap. Here was a beautiful young woman who had entered my life as a scared and troubled teenager. Now she stood before me a strong, confident young lady. Had I done all I could do? Was she ready? Her ship sailed into adulthood and I stood on the shoreline and knew that God would continue to do His work in her life. As most parents do, I prayed that the wind would always be at her back and that she would have smooth sailing. I prayed that her storms would be short and small.

Today Brandi is almost thirty years old. She is married to a fine young man and has four delightful boys. She has sailed in much rough water since she launched out, her storms have been frequent and rough; much of her sailing has been against the wind. Today my prayer is different. I pray that God will give her strength to endure her storms. I pray that she and her family will be drawn closer in relationship to God because of their journey. I pray that the peace of God that passes all understanding will fill her heart and life and bring her joy (Philippians 4:7).

Rebellion or Simple Disagreement?

With each passing year your children gain more independence, and that is how it should be. You want them to be able to stand on their own and to one day get married and have children. They will always need you as their mother—you never outgrow your mom—but *how* they need you will change. As young adults, they need to know that you will love them unconditionally. They will make choices that you disagree with, but that doesn't make them bad kids. Their lives will be different from the one you imagined for them, but that doesn't make you a failure.

I pray that you will really hear me on this one. I talk to so many mothers who feel like their young adults are living in rebellion because they disagree with their choices. But you must make a clear distinction between a rebellious child living outside of the will of God and a young adult who loves God and is trying to be his own person. Just because you disagree with him doesn't mean he is wrong. If you have a young adult who demonstrates his love for God through his life, then be faithful to encourage him and give him your support.

Many young people leave home and put God on the top shelf of their bedroom closet along with an old dusty Bible and a stuffed animal. They see their Christian upbringing as childish and pointless. If your young adult children have a heart for God, rejoice. They may not be as conservative as you are, they may choose to attend a different church, they may let their children do things that you never let them do, but this does not mean they are rebellious or living in sin. Don't have a breakdown; don't think you have failed. They are not going off the deep end; they are just thinking for themselves. They are exercising their right to be different. Allow God to lead them and guide them. If they continue to have a relationship with Him and seek His face, you need not fear.

Blacklisted Children

Through the years I have talked to many young people who are heartbroken because their parents have for all practical purposes disowned them. These are good kids with a heart to follow God and to do the right things.

I remember one young lady who stood in a parking lot and wept as she shared with me that her decision to attend a different church than the one her parents had attended for more than twenty years had sent her father into an outrage. Although she was twenty-two years old at the time, her father asked her to move out. She had been living in an apartment with a friend for six months when I talked to her, but her dad still would not speak to her.

Another girl shared with me how her decision to attend a college that was not on her parents' limited list had put her on the blacklist. She wanted to get a certain degree that was not offered at any of the colleges given as options. Her father refused to help with any of her school bill, although he would have paid the bill in full if she had gone to one of his choices. The tension in the home had grown so great that she finally gave in and went one semester to a school on "the list." She came home at Christmas never to return. By then her resentment and anger at her family had grown out of control. She packed her bags and moved out. On the night I talked to her she was not in church at all, living a pretty wild life, and working at a local hospital as a nurse's aid.

The stories could go on and on. Sadly, so many of these situations could have been avoided if parents had chosen to stand faithfully in support of their young adult. Your young people need you to continue to believe in them even after they are grown and able to make their own decisions. Let the Holy Spirit do His work in their lives. He has promised to faithfully convict them of sin and give them direction.

Don't expect your children to live life just as you have. Don't expect them to make every choice as you would. Remember that God's Word gives us preferences. These affect the choice of music we listen to, the style of church we attend, and a myriad of other options. You might not like their choice of church, but unless the church is preaching another gospel other than Christ crucified, be glad they are going. You will find there are a million things you can find to disagree with them about. I encourage you to ask yourself one question, "Does my young person have a desire to live for God and become more like Him every day?" If you answered that question with a "yes," then praise God for His goodness and encourage them to stay faithful. They might not always do it like you would do it, but in the end God will use them in ways He could have never used you.

Prodigal Sons and Daughters

My heart is also troubled for prodigal sons and daughters. There are so many heartbroken mothers out there with wayward children. It's hard when your child turns a deaf ear to your voice and refuses to heed your warnings. I have talked to kids and wished that I could force them to listen to me. I knew before they walked away that they were not going to do the right thing, and it broke my heart. Many times they would walk away and I would slip off in private and hit my knees. I would lift up their names to God and ask Him to protect them, to get their attention, and to bring them back into a harmonious relationship with Him.

You can't turn your heart away from them when they turn their lives away from God. Wayward sons and daughters need their parents to love them more in their failure than they have ever needed it in their triumphs. When young adults choose to live in a pattern of sin, they alienate themselves from God and from those who love them most. So many mothers I talk to are afraid that giving their wayward child love and attention will be misunderstood as approval of his or her behavior. I don't think this is the case at all. They know you do not approve of their sin, but they need to know that you still love them unconditionally and are there for them. Don't allow them to bring their sin into your home, but make sure they know they are always welcomed.

Call them, write them, invite them over for dinner, continue to keep the connection open, and when the bottom falls out and there is nowhere else to turn, you will probably be the first person they call. Be faithful to pray for them and to be their mom. There is nothing you could do that will help them more.

Detours that Sidetrack Young Adults

As young people step out on their own they will be met with many opportunities to step off the path that God has directed for their lives. Alternate routes are plenteous on their journey. The devil entices them with many new and exciting experiences. It is easy to get caught up in all the new freedom and to make poor choices that will significantly impact their lives. One of the best things a parent can do for their young adults is to prepare them for these enticing rabbit trails.

A common mistake I have watched young adults make is in the area of finances. Materialism can trap so many of them into over-whelming and life-altering debt. Many young adults are not prepared for the responsibility of money. They have never been taught proper stewardship and don't know where to begin in establishing a budget. What they do know is that every credit card company in the world is willing to give them a card and let them spend away. They want to live at the level their parents are living at, but they fail to recognize that their parents have spent a lifetime working to get there. Start early teaching your children the value of money and the importance of saving. As they get older help them to establish a budget and learn to save. This will go a long way when they take those first steps out on their own. It will also keep them from getting into a debt trap that will enslave them.

As young people enter the new world of adulthood they will encounter many new people along the way. Many of these people will introduce your children to a new world of ideas and philosophies. Their worldview will be tested over and over again by those who appear to be intellectual. Talk to them about the importance of discernment as they read and listen to others. The Bible is our guidebook for life. Encourage them to lay all these "new ideas" against the truth of God's Word. For some young people this time period in their lives is a very difficult journey as they sort through what they believe and why. Give them space to talk and process. Your greatest concern is not their questioning but their foundation. The Holy Spirit will do His job and will continue to guide their hearts to truth if they truly desire it. In my experience, I have found that young people who are questioning are thinking and developing a personal worldview, and that is much better than those who never ask. Those who have just adopted the worldview of others without thought or question tend to find it easy to abandon those truths in the end because they never owned them.

Paul wrote, "When I was a child, I spake as a child, I understood as a child, I thought as a child: but when I became a man, I put away childish things" (1 Corinthians 13:11). Immaturity will always seek the easy way, looking to squeeze as much pleasure out of life as possible. Maturity understands that life is a balance of the hard and the easy, and that hard work and discipline bring greater pleasure than frivolity and ease. As your young people grow, you should watch them begin to move from immaturity to maturity. The temptation will always be there to take the shortcuts that life offers. With their new freedom comes new responsibility. This is why when they are teenagers you need to begin to work toward this day. As they demonstrate their capability to handle more responsibility, give them more freedom. I have seen so many young adults with their first taste of real freedom go completely crazy and do things they would never do otherwise. Prepare them for this time of transition and freedom by stretching them as they enter the older teen years. By the time they reach adulthood they should be accustomed to taking responsibility for their actions and making wise choices.

Some young adults abandon everything they know to be good and right because they are enticed by a life they feel they have missed growing up. The music and the lights look inviting. The old ways seem out of date. Church becomes an inconvenience and their relationship with God becomes obsolete. It's easy for this to happen if they are not prepared for the traps. By this time, they should be able to spot them, realize their danger, and be strong enough in their walk with God to avoid them. But as with all of us, sometimes sin gets the best of us.

If you have a child who has been led astray by Satan and is struggling I want you to know this: God is greater. If he is God's child, God will pursue him. If he has never trusted Christ, then Christ is the answer. There is no sin so great that God cannot forgive it, cleanse it, and give us power to overcome it. Don't lose heart. Keep praying and continue loving him. Love him despite all his wrong choices and his sin. Never give up on him. God is still in the miracle-working business. He can take a crooked arrow and make it straight.

Chapter 16

Zulu Time

Seeing the Big Picture

Have you ever wondered why the military uses a different way of telling time than we do in the United States? If you have spent time around military personnel you have probably heard them use phrases like, "I will meet you at 0700," which would mean they would meet you at 7:00 A.M. local time. The military operates on a twenty-four-hour clock, beginning at midnight. So midnight is 0000 hours and you keep adding from there until you get to 11:00 P.M., which would be 2300 hours.

One of my favorite television shows is *JAG*. It was a show about the Judge Advocate General and his personnel. At the beginning of the show, the time and location would flash across the bottom of the screen so you would know when and where the scene you were watching was happening. One term that was attached to the time was "Zulu." I often wondered what in the world Zulu was and what it had to do with the time. Curiosity got the best of me and I looked it up.

The military uses the twenty-four-hour clock because its dealings are worldwide. Since the military must coordinate with bases in other time zones they need to make sure that they don't get confused on what time zone they are referring to. For the military it is vital that everyone worldwide is on the same time so it can coordinate its efforts. For all operational matters they use the time in Greenwich,

England (Greenwich Mean Time—GMT). The military refers to this time as Zulu Time. They do this by dividing the world up into 24 times zones and then attaching a letter of the alphabet to represent each zone. The time zone for Greenwich, England, has been assigned the letter "Z." The military uses its phonetic alphabet and calls it Zulu. The National Weather Service and many other agencies use Zulu time to correctly identify the exact time needed. The United States and Canada are two of the few countries that do not use the military time clock to state their time.

So what time is it in your home? I live in Chattanooga, Tennessee, which is in the Eastern Time Zone, so right now it's 11:15 A.M. Chattanooga is my home, it's my comfort zone, it's the place I love to be, but I have to be careful that it never becomes my world. Fortunately, God has blessed me with a ministry in which I travel. I constantly have to think about other time zones, other states, other places, and other people. I am so grateful for that because if I am not careful it is easy to become settled in my little world and never give the rest of the world a thought. It may be Eastern Standard Time on my watch, but it better be Zulu time in my heart.

I need to see the big picture as God sees it—a world full of people from different places, different cultures, different creeds, and many on different sides of the globe, and yet Christ died for all of them. We are not training our children to be good little boys and girls just for the sake of being good. Each of them has a purpose and God has a mission for their lives. We want them to follow the commands of God and walk in a relationship with Him so they can fulfill the mission and reach the goals that God has set for them.

Do you see the big picture as you go about your daily routine? Are you helping your children think globally? Do you believe your children realize that there is a world out there with all sorts of exciting opportunities for them?

I grew up in a small town in North Carolina. By the time I graduated from high school I had been as far west as Texas, as far north as New York, and as far south as Florida. Most of the young people my age had not been that far. Life was simple where I was raised. You graduated from high school and either got married and got a local job or went to a college close by and then got married and got a local job. So when I graduated with my master's degree and headed off to Wisconsin for my first job people thought I was crazy. That was almost twenty-five years ago, but even today when I go back home to visit I almost never leave without someone asking when I am going to move home. When I tell them I don't know, they just shake their heads and smile. They have come to understand that I operate on Zulu time.

It's easy to grow complacent and comfortable in our little worlds. If we are not careful, the world around us changes but we stay the same. Many adults don't like change. We are afraid of what change may mean to our lives and our comfort zones. If we are not careful these fears will be passed on to our children.

My grandfather was the treasurer for a very large church for over thirty years. He did all his work by hand and relied on his very large adding machine for accurate numbers. The church offered to buy him a computer but Grandaddy didn't want one. He just didn't trust them and he didn't want to learn how to use one. Grandaddy has been in heaven for several years now and a computer sits in the place of his old adding machine. Time and technology have moved on.

Technology has brought the world together in a way we never thought possible. So many young people have their finger on the pulse of technology and realize how much potential is there. It's time we as adults broaden our vision and help our young people dream big dreams. There is still so much to do.

There is still a huge core of the population who have never heard the gospel. The 10/40 Window is a section of our globe that extends from ten degrees to forty degrees north of the equator, West Africa to East Asia. The majority of the world's Muslims, Hindus, and Buddhists live in this region. The statistics regarding this area of the world are startling:

- Two-thirds of the world's population (more than 3.2 billion) live in the 10/40 Window.
- 97 percent of the least evangelized countries are in the 10/40 Window.
- 82 percent of the world's poorest people live in the 10/40 Window.

- The majority of the world's megacities (those with a population of more than one million) are in the 10/40 Window.
- 95 percent of the people living in the 10/40 Window are unevangelized. (Many have never heard the gospel message even once.)
- Only 1.25 percent of mission giving is going to missionaries in the 10/40 Window.[29]

There is a world out there that desperately needs believers in Christ to wake up, get up, and make a difference. Young people who know Jesus Christ cannot be content to sit back and stare at the television or the computer. They cannot think the world's greatest problems revolve around them. They must live on Zulu time. They must understand that in order to impact their world they will have to think differently than the average teenager. Their attitudes and actions will have to be globally influenced. They must realize that for them to touch a lost and dying world they will need to coordinate their efforts with many time zones in mind. There is no room for prejudice.

God will not call every child to make a difference in the 10/40 Window or to go into missions or even full-time Christian work for that matter. We need doctors, lawyers, factory workers, and teachers. We need politicians, nurses, and flight attendants. It doesn't matter what vocation your child chooses, but it needs to be a job he can use for the glory of God. God uses all types of people in all different places to reach the world.

Outward Focus, Global Impact

It's easy to become consumed with our own little worlds. We all have problems and circumstances that are more than we can handle. Most days we do well if we survive. Jesus promised more. In John 10:10, He promised an abundant life to those who follow Him. In John 15, He promised a fruitful life to those who would engraft their life in Him. Jesus was all about living life to its fullest. He told us that in this world we would have troubles but that He had come to overcome the world (John 16:33). He promised more. In fact, in Luke 6:38, He promised an overflowing abundance that we cannot measure. However, that abundance is based on one key concept: as you give so will it be given to you. Jesus said that if you focus your life on others and give to them, He will pour back into your life the same size cup you used to give to others. But Jesus went on in verse 39 to illustrate this point with a parable. "Can the blind lead the blind? Shall not they both fall into the ditch?" Jesus explained that the student is not above his teacher, if the teacher is fit to serve others, the student will follow.

Moms, I hope you know that your children are watching you and following you. They will tend to have the same focus you have. If you are going to raise children who are selfless and giving, then you have to be that way yourself. Children need to see their parents demonstrating a care and concern for others that goes beyond the ordinary. Giving money is good and we should do that, but giving money is the easiest way to give. There are times when we need to give of our time and ourselves. I know of several families who spend part of their Thanksgiving Day at the local rescue missions and homeless shelters helping to feed those who are less fortunate. Their children are learning so many important life lessons when they roll up their own sleeves and get involved.

Grayson Rosenberger is a wonderful example of a teen who was affected by his parents' work with the less fortunate. Grayson's mother lost both of her legs to a car accident, and as a result she started a non-profit organization called Standing with Hope. Grayson's parents have dedicated their lives to working with prosthetic patients in Africa. They see their mission "to provide hope to others ... and to share Christ." Grayson's parents told him about a boy they had met in Africa named Daniel. Daniel had broken his leg playing soccer and had to have it amputated. The basic metal-rod prosthetic leg given to Daniel worked fine, but the kids made fun of him. He wanted a covering but they were too expensive.

Fifteen-year-old Grayson began to think about how he could help Daniel. He wanted to invent an inexpensive leg covering that would work. Sealed Air Corporation was having a Bubble Wrap Invention Competition and Daniel found out. He entered the contest with a prosthetic leg covering he had made out of heated bubble wrap. The invention was a success and Grayson won the contest. Last June, Grayson and his parents traveled back to Ghana to visit

Daniel and give him his leg covering. Sadly enough, Daniel had died ten days earlier from malaria. Determined to stay the course, Grayson remolded the covering for another boy. For the next ten days Grayson and his parents fitted over twenty-five people with new legs and trained the local clinic workers on how to build Grayson's invention.[30] Inspired and encouraged by his parents' example, Grayson went on to do great works of kindness himself.

The Ugliness of Prejudice

Regardless of what part of the country you are in, you will find prejudice, either against the color of a person's skin, the accent of a person's speech, or the values of a person's life. It is hard for me to comprehend how people who claim to love the Lord show hatred for people who don't fit their mold. Jesus did not judge a person based on the color of his skin, the part of the country he lived in, or the amount of money in his pocket. He did not turn away from those who were downtrodden or being accused of some sin. In fact, over and over again in the Gospels Jesus reminds us that He died for all men and He came to reach those who were at their lowest.

The Pharisees hated Jesus for His unselfish love because it stood out in such glaring opposition to all they believed in. The Pharisees were religious, but they had no time for those who were poor and could not support their cause. They had no time for those who were not of Jewish descent and ancestry. They despised sinners and boasted of their perfection in the keeping of the law. Jesus condemned them and gave His most scathing words of judgment to them. Jesus loved people; the Pharisees loved themselves.

I wish God's people could understand how greatly they are sinning before Him when they allow prejudice to enter their hearts and affect their actions. A person who holds this ill will toward others will never be able to be used by God to reach the world. It's time we stop blaming our hometown, our relatives, and our past for our sin. If not we will pass this same heritage along to our children, and the cycle will never be broken. The jokes, the slang, and the arrogance need to be laid on the altar. We need to ask God to give us a love for others of every race and creed. We need to pray for a broken heart for those chained by sin. And we need to allow those who claim the name of Christ and do it differently than we do to be judged by God, not us.

All the Children of the World

Remember that sweet children's song: "Jesus loves the little children, all the children of the world"? Don't just sing it; *teach* your children to love other nationalities, races, and creeds. Teach them to pray for people all around the world. I would encourage you to get a globe and teach your children about the world. Read them stories of missionaries and pray for them by name. As they grow older talk to them about the orphans scattered across the globe due to AIDS.

For the past few years Dare for More Ministries has supported a young person through Compassion International. I am able to correspond with this young girl on a monthly basis. Anitha is from an AIDS-infected area in Rwanda. It has been a blessing for me to know that we are making a difference in one life. Maybe your family could support a child in another country. What a great way to expose your children to a world very different from their own.

Remember compassion starts at home. Having a heart for others should start right in our own communities. Jesus started His earthly ministry in the communities and towns around Him, and when He gave the disciples the Great Commission He started in the areas closest to home and moved out to include the uttermost parts of the world. Maybe your children will have the opportunity to impact the world one day, but that day will never happen unless they start at home. Teach them what it means to live with other people in mind. Help them step out of their comfort zones by giving of their time and effort to those who are in need. Point out the blessings and the joys that come with putting God first, others second, and yourself last. Stretch their vision beyond their backyard.

Amy Carmichael, missionary to India, said it well, "You can give without loving. But you cannot love without giving." Teach your children to give of themselves, regardless of how little they think they have to give, and watch God give the increase. In God's economy it only takes a little boy willing to give his few fish and slices of bread to feed thousands. God is global; He has His hand on the pulse of the world. His vision is not limited to distance, space, or time; nor is His ability limited by our talents or efforts. He is looking for Christians who live in Zulu time, who have a global vision to do His work. Prepare your children for His service, and their lives will never be richer.

Chapter 17

Semper Fidelis

Always Faithful

The Marine Corps has a single motto that defines their way of life—Semper Fidelis. The phrase is in Latin and it simply means "Always Faithful." Since 1883 this motto has encouraged Marines to remain faithful to each mission, to their fellow Marines, to the Corps, and to their country. It is a motto that describes a brotherhood that lasts for a lifetime. Former Marine Cam Beck put it this way, "It isn't 'Sometimes Faithful.' Nor is it 'Usually Faithful,' but always. It is not negotiable. It is not relative but absolute."[31]

A Faithful God

As I pondered how to end this journey that we have embarked on together, I thought about this simple motto and the power behind it. "Always Faithful." It conjures up so many strong images in my mind. Immediately I think about my God who is always faithful. Deuteronomy says He is the faithful God who keeps His covenant (7:9). First Corinthians describes Him as faithful in providing an escape from temptation (10:13). The book of Revelation gives us His name as "Faithful and True" (19:11). God is faithful—He is *always* faithful.

Each and every one of us is encouraged and strengthened by knowing that God will always be true to His Word and to His promises. I especially appreciate God's faithfulness when I am presented with a hard task or great responsibility, for I know that I don't have the ability or the wisdom needed, but God does.

Mothers, God has called you to a great task, and because He has called you He will be faithful to help you complete it (1 Thessalonians 5:24). God has not called you to do anything He has not equipped you to do. Your kids may be giving you a hard time and you may feel like they are going to be the death of you, but God knew just what they needed. He matched up the perfect mother for each child, and He will provide you with the strength and willpower to strap your boots on for another day.

I gain so much from going through the Bible and finding the things that God has promised me. Wisdom, strength, companionship, direction, discernment, and much more are mine for the asking. So when you feel like giving up and giving in—don't! Seek the face of the Faithful One. Ask Him to help you get through. Ask for His blessing and provision. Ask for your miracle. Many times we don't have because we don't ask (James 4:2).

A Faithful Follower

As God is faithful to you, it is your turn to demonstrate His faithfulness to your children. You may have never been a Marine, but your motto must be the same. "Always Faithful." Your children must know that they can count on you. They need you to be faithful to God. Keep your relationship with Him the top priority in your life. Make time to go to God in prayer, sit at His feet, and learn from Him.

Your children need to see a faithful example of a mother who is in love with Jesus. Too many times our children equate working for Jesus as relationship. What we do for God is important but cannot equal the personal walk that we have with Him. Show your children a woman who is not as much about *doing* for God as she is about *being* with God. Our focus should be on our relationship with God, and He will direct our "to do" list.

As your children watch you prioritize your relationship with Christ they will be affected personally. Your faithfulness through good times and bad will speak volumes to them about their own walk with God. It's not about being perfect. It's about getting up every day and living a life of passion for Christ. People are more impressed by faithfulness than perfection. If you are perfect then no one can relate to you, but if you are imperfect and strive to always be faithful, then you have my attention because I can relate to striving imperfection.

A Faithful Wife

If you are married, be faithful to your husband. Making your marriage a priority is very important for the health and well-being of your children. Your kids need to see a healthy and loving marriage relationship modeled. This will help them feel secure, as well as teach them how marriages work. Guard yourself against adultery by setting up boundaries of protection in your life and marriage.

If you are unsure how to set boundaries I would like to recommend Jerry Jenkins' book *Hedges*. In this book he teaches couples how to protect their marriage. One of his boundaries concerns flirting. Be careful not to flirt, or get emotionally involved with a man who is not your husband. If you and your husband are struggling don't share that with another man, unless he is a relative. Guard your testimony and your heart by avoiding situations that would cause others to question your integrity. According to research, children who are raised by their own married parents "live longer, are physically healthier, and show fewer signs of emotional distress and mental illness."[32]

One of the best things you can do for your children is to make your marriage a priority. Love your husband and make time for him. Even adult children feel the impact of a marriage that is not working. I realize that not everything is within your control, but do your part to be a faithful wife.

If you have been through a divorce you can still demonstrate faithfulness as you forgive wrongs that were done to you, as you refuse to talk evil of their dad regardless of his issues, and as you ask for forgiveness for your mistakes. As you model a Christlike faithfulness it will help your children heal and move on. Your faithfulness to do what is right in difficult times can be such a valuable learning experience for your children, regardless of their age.

What Does Faithfulness Look Like?

I looked up the word *faithful* in the dictionary and found these definitions: unwavering in belief, consistently loyal, not adulterous or promiscuous, conscientious, correct, reliable. Faithful is quite a demanding word. It implies character and values. It's not a word that should be used flippantly. There is a dignity that comes with its use that gives immediate respect to the person that it's describing.

The Marine Corps picked an ambitious word to be its motto. If each Marine truly lives out the motto of Semper Fi then they will represent our country and the Corps well. In order to accomplish this grand goal, the Marine Corps uses several visual symbols to enforce their concept of faithfulness. The Corps also has a set of core values that each Marine is asked to memorize and live by.

Symbols of Faithfulness

For the Marines the symbols are simple, but they represent all that the Corps entails. It starts with their emblem: the eagle, globe, and anchor. The eagle represents our nation, the globe represents the world, and the anchor stands for the naval tradition of the Marine Corps. In the air, on land, and at sea, the Marines' worldwide presence is dedicated to protecting our nation. New recruits are given this emblem when they finish Recruit Training. It is a symbol that they are now United States Marines.

The second symbol of a Marine is the dress blues, a uniform that is hard to miss. From the red piping on the dark jacket to the gold buttons that bear the eagle, globe, and anchor, the Marine Corps dress uniform conveys dignity. When dress blues are issued, each Marine is given strict regulations regarding the wearing of the uniform. The standards are high, and each Marine is expected to abide by them.

The next symbol is the sword signifying the Marine Corps heritage as "America's original protectors." Marine officers carry the Mameluke sword, dating all the way back to 1805 when a Mameluke chieftain in North Africa gave it to a Marine lieutenant for marching his troops over six hundred miles to help protect them.

The Marine Corps flag is the banner under which the few and the proud live, fight, and die. The flag incorporates all the pieces into one. The eagle, globe, and anchor are centered on a background of scarlet. A ribbon hangs out of the mouth of the eagle bearing the motto "Semper Fidelis." This ever-present symbol can be found in the offices of the President of the United States, the Secretary of Defense, the Secretary of the Navy, and the Chairman and Vice Chairman of the Joint Chiefs of Staff.

The Marines have learned that if their motto is ever going to be lived out, it must be more than words. In your family, *faithfulness* must be more than just a word. Even though the word paints a grand picture, it will never be fully realized in the lives of your children if it remains an adjective.

Every family has symbols in their own home that represent who they are and what they stand for. If you had to design an emblem that would represent who you are, where you have been, and where you are going, what would it look like? You are passing down a heritage to your children. I am afraid many parents have not put a lot of thought into what they are leaving to their children. When most people think of passing something down they think of their inheritance: grandpa's watch, the antique desk, and some money. Heritage is more than just things; it's values, character, honor, tradition, and much more. What are you passing down? Some parents pass down a tradition of bitterness and anger, others a life of resentment and unforgiveness. Mom, what symbols represent your life? Like it or not, your children are being affected by them.

Over and over again in the Old Testament God warned Israel that their sin would affect generations to come—and it did. Israel continually turned to idols as a form of worship and their children were affected. The unbelief of the parents was passed down to their children, and each generation was worse than the one before. By the time the Old Testament comes to an end, Israel as a whole is steeped in idolatry and judgment.

Evaluate your children's heritage and make sure you are providing symbols to guide them and to remind them of what is important. In the beginning of the book of Joshua, God's people were getting ready to cross over the Jordan River and enter the land of promise. It had been a long time coming and they were anxious to move forward. As they entered the Jordan, God made the waters to stand up on each side, just as He had done for their parents at the

Red Sea. After they had crossed over, God asked Joshua to bring twelve large stones out of the middle of the Jordan River and bring them into camp. These stones were to serve as a reminder of what had happened that day. Some day their children would ask what the memorial stones were all about, and for generations to come each father and mother would be able to tell their children about the day God moved the waters so their family could cross over into promise land (Joshua 4:1–24).

When God does something wonderful and miraculous for your family, take the time to make memorial stones. Even if the symbol is simple, it is a lasting testament of the goodness of God to your family.

In my journal I have a bank statement taped to a page as a memorial stone. I went through a very tough time financially early in my ministry. I honestly didn't know how it would ever work out. From my perspective it seemed overwhelming. But little by little, God proved Himself faithful to me. He was working all things out for my good, but I could not see it. As I tried to walk in obedience, He provided. The day I taped that statement in my journal, I was debt free and had more money in my checking account than bills due. Oh, I wasn't rich by any means, but God had brought me through a deep valley and I just had to make sure I never forgot it. That bank statement was a symbol of His faithfulness to me in good times and bad.

Take some time to think about what God has done for you and your family. Do your children realize how God has worked on their behalf? If not, they should. Make it a habit to erect some memorial stones for your family so even when the little ones get older and ask you will be able to tell them about how good God has been to your family.

A family creed, a particular symbol, or a motto, are all good reminders to your children of the importance of certain values and character traits. You might get creative and come up with your own emblem, symbol, or motto.

Some of you may grimace when you think of your heritage. When you think back to your family experience your memories are painful and ones you wish you could forget. You may feel as if you have nothing worthwhile to pass on to your children. I talk to many women who have been saved from a very sinful past. They are afraid they are incapable of helping their children find a better way. I want to assure you that God is not limited by your sin or by your past. It doesn't matter how bad you have been or how bad your background has been. God can work through your life to start a new heritage for your family.

You have the wonderful opportunity to stop the cycle of destruction and begin a new heritage that your great grandchildren will bless you for. Maybe you feel as if the flag flying over your home has been anger; let's take that flag down and put up patience and love. If the emblem of your life is filled with sin, then ask God for His forgiveness and ask Him to help you pass on something holy to your children. Set out to fill your home with symbols that remind your children of their godly heritage.

Proverbs 31 describes a woman who was faithful to serve the Lord and her family, and it says that her children rose up and called her blessed and her husband praised her. Can the average woman ever attain to this example? To be honest, I don't think the average woman can, but I do think that a woman filled with the power of God can live an above-average life. Sadly, too many of us are not living by the power of God. Instead we are opting to live by the power of self. I have learned the hard way that there is very little power there and in the end it only leads to a life that is way below average.

It's time mothers rose up and decided that through the power of God they can claim a new heritage for their family. Don't ask yourself what everyone else is doing. Don't find the best mother you know and try to imitate her. Ask God to help you to rise above the status quo. Ask Him to empower you to be the best mother you can be for His glory.

Don't assume that the woman in Proverbs 31 was a woman with unattainable superhero qualities; assume she was a normal woman who had a passion for Christ, her husband, and her children, and she just wouldn't let the devil get in her way. I don't think she was placed in Scripture to give us a set pattern to follow. I believe she was put there to show us as women that when we are filled with God's power, we can be more and do more than we ever dreamed possible. Let this woman be an inspiration for you to set the bar higher and dream big for you and your family. Nothing is impossible with God.

I realize that we will probably pass along some traits to our children that we regret. This is another reason it is so important to place reminders in their paths. They need to know that they can deal with their issues as well, and God can purify their lives. There is hope for your family. The woman in Proverbs 31 has often been called the "Virtuous Woman." I can imagine no greater heritage to pass along to your children than a mother who lives a life of virtue.

Core Values

In the end it takes more than dress blues, a sword, and a flag to make a Marine. What really counts is a person's actions. Marines pride themselves on being the first on the scene, the first to help, and the first into battle. They hold high the values of honor, courage, and commitment. These standards guide their actions on land, in air, and at sea, in combat, and at home.

I want you to embrace these same values of honor, courage, and commitment. When I think about the battle for the hearts and lives of our children, I am often overwhelmed. I find my mind sprinting from one thought to the next and I wonder where to start. Often I find myself asking God to settle my heart and mind and give me clarity to focus. If I am not careful in my attempt to solve it all in one fatal swoop, I end up stirring up a lot of dust and accomplishing nothing. I found myself feeling the same way as I sat down to pen these words. There are so many needs and so much to be done. As I prayed and asked God for a way to bring it down to a simple concept, He reminded me of the Marine's core values and of His own. For the Marines it's honor, courage, and commitment. For God it's love.

A lawyer once came to Jesus and asked him what was the greatest commandment in the whole law. There were so many laws that the Pharisees were sure this would be an impossible question for Jesus to answer. How could He pick one over the other? Jesus gave the man a simple answer, "Thou shalt love the Lord thy God with all thy heart, and with all thy soul, and with all thy mind. This is the first and great commandment. And the second is like unto it, Thou shalt love thy neighbour as thyself. On these two commandments hang all the law and the prophets" (Matthew 22:37–38).

Jesus understood what the Pharisees did not: if you truly loved God you would follow all His commands, and if you truly loved your neighbor you would treat him in a Christlike manner. By being obedient to these two laws, you automatically obey the others. Every law can be placed under one of these two headings.

God gave me so much clarity as I thought about these simple but difficult concepts. Reaching our young people is a difficult task. When you think about all that you want for them it is definitely overwhelming. So where do you start? How can you boil it all down to something you can get your arms around?

First, we must live out biblical core values for our young people to see. Make a decision to love God with all your heart, soul, and mind. Then decide to love others as you love yourself. Putting your love for God first and your love for your family next will ensure that you leave them an example to follow and a heritage to claim. It's impossible to be loved so much and not be forever changed by that love. God's love changes us, and your love can change your children. Once you get your love right, then the rest of these core values should follow.

Second, we must live out a life of honor. Live to the highest standards ethically and morally. Proverbs 22:4 says, "By humility and the fear of the Lord are riches, and honour, and life." Live a life of honor.

Third, we must live a life of courage. As the Marines say, "Courage is not the absence of fear. It is the ability to face fear and overcome it." God has given all of us the courage we need to face the toughest of obstacles. I find great courage as I listen to mothers tell me their stories. Mothers have the ability to muster up the courage to do the hard things at the most difficult moments. "Have not I commanded thee? Be strong and of a good courage; be not afraid, neither be thou dismayed: for the Lord thy God is with thee whithersoever thou goest" (Joshua 1:9).

Fourth, we must demonstrate commitment. Commitment is a dedication that you will not quit. It's a promise you have made to yourself and to your children to show up and make a difference. Commitment calls you to a higher standard and personifies a spirit of determination. Your commitment to God, your husband, and your children must be your number one priority. Without commitment you will never be faithful. For many women *commitment* is a hard word. Sometimes it triggers negative feelings and memories of someone who broke a promise. *Commitment* is not only a hard word, but it can be a scary word. Commitment has the ring of "forever" to it. It implies a decision that will last for a lifetime. Commitment should never be entered into lightly, but once you're in, commit to stay. God attaches a very special promise when we commit to Him. "Commit thy way unto the LORD; trust also in him; and he shall bring it to pass" (Psalm 37:5).

These are simple core values that carry great weight. As you dedicate yourself to these values in your personal life, then you must also instill them in your children. As they hear your words, watch your walk, and follow your instructions, they begin to manifest these values in their own life. God will give them the power to raise the bar in their own life.

Life will test them. It always does. The Marines create their own trial by fire to make sure that each recruit has learned these values. The Crucible is the last test a recruit will have to pass before he is officially called a Marine. For fifty-four hours every value that the recruit has been taught will be tested. During this test of physical, mental, and emotional endurance the recruits will get only eight hours of sleep and march about forty miles. Each segment of the test requires a demonstration of the values they have learned and their ability to become a member of a team. No one gets through the Crucible alone. The Crucible reveals what it is designed to reveal, whether a person is ready for the real battle.

The test is designed to end at sunrise. Then the recruits—exhausted and hungry—finish the Crucible by marching into the parade grounds. They stand at attention in front of a replica of the Iwo Jima Memorial, and there a color guard raises the American flag. After a prayer, the first sergeant addresses them, and they are given their own insignia—the eagle, globe, and anchor. The drill instructor then shakes their hands and calls them "Marine" for the first time.[33]

I cannot help but think of the all the crucibles that God has allowed me to go through. He has used each of those training exercises in my life to solidify my core values. As I pass these tests and gain strength from them I look more like Him than ever before.

God allows trials to come in our lives for many reasons, but if He allows pain you can be assured it has a purpose. Job, who underwent testing that few of us will experience, realized that it had a purpose. In Job 23:10 he makes a remarkable statement: "But he knoweth the way that I take: when he hath tried me, I shall come forth as gold." Our core values will be tested, and our children will also face their own trials and tests. It is for these days that we train and prepare.

If my core values are not what they should be, I falter and fail the test. Testing reveals what is really inside of a person. As you raise your children their core will be revealed. You will know if they are battle ready or not. Stay with them, don't give up, and don't let them quit. Keep preparing, training, working, and praying until they get it.

For parents there is no training course on raising children. Moms don't get to practice, but they are tested. You don't get to practice on someone else's kids before you have your own. Moms have a baby and beg God to help them figure it out as they go. The great thing about that is that God takes you through your own personal trials to prepare you for all of life, even parenting. He even gives you an internal guide called the Holy Spirit to help you along each step of the way.

Moms would make good Marines. The Crucible does not intimidate moms because they have completed that test many times. Rarely eating, losing sleep, walking the floors at all hours of the night—this is all in a day's work for a mother. There should be a monument for mothers, a place where everyone who has ever been touched by a mother can come and pay tribute. But you will probably never get a tickertape parade in your honor. I doubt a flag will ever be designed to symbolize all you are and all you mean, although good mothers deserve that and so much more. A mother's emblem is her love, her hugs, and her support, for it is these things that leave a mark on the world. A mother's flag is her children, unfurling to reveal all that she has worked so hard to protect. Although a monument would be nice, most mothers I talk to don't need a monument in their honor. At the end of the day a godly mother will rejoice if her children grow up to love God with all their heart, soul, mind, and strength.

God has given you an amazing opportunity to impact lives, and if you have taken that opportunity to heart then you have earned the title of mother.

You've Earned It

For every long night bathing the warm head of your sick child,
You've earned your title.
For every diaper you've changed,
For every nose you've wiped,
You've earned your title.
For every lunch you've packed,
For every "boo-boo" you've kissed,
For every spill you've cleaned,
You've earned your title.
For every funeral you've conducted for a pet,
For every time you've listened when no one else cared,
For every monster you have chased from the room,
For every booked you've read,
You've earned your title.
For every time you left the night light on,
For every time you didn't tell Dad,
For every music recital, ballgame and event you've attended,
For every time you sat in the passenger side in fear,
For every picture you took along the way,
You've earned your title.
For every time you've cheered,
For every cookie you have baked,
For every party you have thrown,
For every toy you have sacrificed for,
For every secret you have kept,
For every project you helped create,
For every tear you have wiped,
You've earned your title.
Your title is Mom.
It represents all you have meant to those who have depended so
    much on you.
It represents your love, sacrifice and dedication.

You mean a thousand things to each child
So when you hear your title called,
Stand tall, be proud,
You've earned it.

One day Christians will stand before the judgment seat of Christ and give account for their lives. What we did on this earth and why we did it will be tested by fire. Only the actions and motives that were true and pure will come through the fire. Everything we did for our own selfish ambition will be burned up with nothing to show for it.

There are many amazing people who have walked this globe and many have felt their impact. I am sure you could come up with a list of people that you feel will come forth as gold. But I wonder if we will be surprised to hear those great people's mothers called up first. Women who have prayed, modeled, instructed, and poured everything into their children, their names unknown to the world, but known by God. They have impacted the world because they influenced their children.

For years thoughts have spun through my head, thoughts that I wanted to share with mothers and fathers alike. As time has gone by my passion has only intensified for increasing awareness and fervency in action. It's time we stop talking about the problems and start doing something about them. There are really only two choices: sit back and hope it all works out; or get up, lace up your boots, get in the action, and fight for what is important to you.

Every day in our country people fight for what they believe in. Some lie in front of bulldozers in order to save a small bird's habitat because they believe it's important. Some drive hundreds of miles, carry signs and banners, and march for a cause. And some lay down their very lives to protect the people they love and the country they live in. Our country is full of people willing to stand for what they believe in and fight for its survival, right or wrong.

How about you? Are you willing to sacrifice your life for your children's? You can relax, because I am not asking you if you would die for your children, although I am sure that many of you would. What I am asking is—will you live for them? Will you sacrifice for them, fight for them, and refuse to let them be captured by the enemy?

God gave them to you. He knew that you were the perfect person for each of them. He entrusted their lives into your hands for a little while. No mother understood this more than Mary, the mother of Jesus. His birth turned her world upside down. For twelve years she held Him, nurtured Him, and cared for His every need. It would take a trip to Jerusalem for Mary to realize that her days in that capacity were numbered.

I can imagine a caravan of people: cousins, aunts, and uncles from every side of the family tree taking the long trip home from Jerusalem. With so many relatives to play with and so many adults to keep an eye out, Mary and Joseph just assumed Jesus was among the group. But as they began to ask around, they suddenly realized that no one had seen Jesus since yesterday in Jerusalem. Frantically, Mary and Joseph made the day's journey back to the city. They could only hope He was safe. After three days of agony, Mary and Joseph entered the Temple and found Jesus sitting among the teachers of the law listening and asking questions. With relief, Mary questioned Jesus about why He stayed behind. Did He not realize that they had been worried about Him?

Jesus asked Mary why they were looking for Him, and why they were so worried; didn't they realize He was doing the very thing that He came to earth to do? Although Mary didn't understand that day, she spent a lot of time thinking about His words (Luke 2:41–52). As the days passed she realized that her Son was just on loan to her from God. His purpose was much bigger than just Nazareth.

I hope you have the vision to see the big picture when it comes to your children. They are just on loan to you from God. Although they will forever be your children, they have been ordained from the beginning for a higher purpose. Their lives are meant to impact the world. Each of their assignments will be different. Some will touch many, some will touch few, but each of them have their calling. It's not your job to call them, but it is your job to make sure they are ready to answer the call.

One night the little boy Samuel thought he heard someone calling his name. He got up from bed, went to Eli, the priest, and asked if he had called. After several times of this, Eli realized that God was calling the young boy's name. He told Samuel that the next time he heard his name called to say, "Speak Lord, for thy servant heareth" (1 Samuel 3:9). Sure enough, Samuel heard his name again and answered God's call. That night God began to speak to Samuel and use him to help His chosen people, Israel. Out of all the prophets, Samuel is the one whose life we know the most about. God used him in a mighty way.

Samuel had a wonderful mother named Hannah. Hannah prayed for a son and promised the Lord if He answered her prayer she would give him back to God. Although she only had a short time to raise Samuel, she impacted his life to answer the call of God.

Like Samuel, your children were born with a calling and a purpose. I pray that you will have the vision to see the potential of your children for advancing God's kingdom, the wisdom to instruct them in righteousness, the courage to train them for battle, and the love to send them out into the care of Him who is called Faithful and True. I pray that until that day, you will take their calling seriously enough to grab your boots, lace them up, and fearlessly march on. And one day, when God says "well done" over your life, I pray that you will hear your children loudly proclaim, "That's my Mama, yep, the one in the combat boots."

End Notes

[1] Jacob Brown to the Secretary of War, 1825, in "American State Papers," *Military Affairs* 3, 111.

[2] Brenda Hunter, *The Power of Mother Love* (Colorado Springs: Waterbrook Press), back cover.

[3] Josh McDowell, *How to Help Your Child Say "No" to Sexual Pressure* (Waco: Word Publishing, 1987), 19.

[4] Beth Reece, "Warrior Transition Course," About.com: http://usmilitary.about.com/od/armyjoin/a/warriortransit.htm (March 8, 2005).

[5] Alex and Brett Harris, The Rebelution, http://www.therebelution.com/about/rebelution.htm 2006 (December 11, 2008).

[6] Dean Smith and Gerald Bell with John Kilgo, *The Carolina Way* (New York: Penguin Press, 2004), 135.

[7] Andy Stanley, *Louder Than Words* (Sisters, Ore.: Multnomah, 2004), 31.

[8] Charles Swindoll, *Strengthening Your Grip* (Waco, Tex.: Word Books, 1982), 207.

[9] Substance Abuse and Mental Health Services Administration (SAMHSA), National Survey on Drug Use and Health (2006).

[10] L. D. Johnston, P. M. O'Malley, J. G. Bachman, and J. E. Schulenberg, "Data Tables from the 2007 Monitoring the Future Survey," *University of Michigan News and Information Services*, www.monitoringthefuture.org (2007).

[11] Substance Abuse and Mental Health Services Administration (SAMHSA), The NSDUH Report: Out of Home Services for Emotional or Behavioral Problems Among Youth Ages 12 to 17: 2002 to 2006 (September 18, 2008).

[12]Substance Abuse and Mental Health Services Administration (SAMHSA), Parent Awareness of Youth Use of Cigarettes, Alcohol, and Marjiuana (April 24, 2008).

[13]Family Safe Media, Pornography Statistics, 2007, www. familysafemedia.com (November 18, 2008).

[14]Josh McDowell, "American Demographics Report," Josh McDowell Ministry. http://www.josh.org/site/c.ddKDIMNtEqG/b.4167343/apps/s/content.asp?ct=5486545 (accessed November 15, 2009).

[15]Stephen Covey, *The Seven Habits of Highly Effective People* (New York: Fireside, 1989).

[16]Jimmy Johnson, *Perfect Love* (Indianapolis, Ind.: Wesley, 1987).

[17]Michael Winerip, "Phelps's Mother Recalls Helping Her Son Find Gold Medal Focus," *New York Times*: http://www.nytimes.com/2008/08/10/sports/olympics/10Rparent.html?_r=2&oref=slogin&oref=slogin (August 8, 2008).

[18]Judy Dutton, "ADHD Parenting Advice from Michael Phelps' Mom," *ADDITUDE*, http://www.additudemag.com/adhd/article/1998.html (April/May, 2007).

[19]Carol Burnett and Bernard Klein, *One More Time: A Memoir* (New York: Random House, 2003).

[20]"How To: Tips for Targeting Tweens," Marketing Vox (July 30, 2008). http://www.marketingvox.com/how-to-tips-for-targeting-tweens-040147/?camp=newsletter&src=mv&type=textlink (accessed December 3, 2008).

[21]Nielsen Media Research, "35% of U.S. Tweens Own a Mobile Phone, According to Nielsen," *Nielsen Media* (December 3, 2007). http://www.nielsenmedia.com/nc/portal/site/Public/menuitem.55dc65b4a7d5adff3f65936147a062a0/?vgnextoid=885472b6caf96110VgnVCM100000ac0a260aRCRD (accessed December 3, 2008).

[22]Kay S. Hymowitz, "Tweens: Ten Going on Sixteen," *City Journal*, edited by Brian C. Anderson, Manhattan Institute (Autumn 1998). http://www.city-journal.org/html/8_4_a1.html (accessed December 4, 2008).

[23]Ibid.

[24]Ibid.

[25]Women in Military Service for America Memorial Foundation, Inc. "Highlights in the History of Military Women," *Women's Memorial*, http://www.womensmemorial.org/Education/timeline. html (accessed November 10, 2009).

[26]Steve Biddulph, *Raising Boys: Why Boys Are Different and How to Help Them Become Happy and Well-Raised Men*, 2nd edition (Berkeley, Calif.: Celestial Arts, 2008).

[27]Paul Gericke, *Crucial Experiences in the Life of D. L. Moody* (Insight Press Inc, 1978).

[28]Laura Sessions Stepp, "Study: Half of All Teens Have Had Oral Sex," *The Washington Post* (September 16, 2005), http://www.washingtonpost.com/wp-dyn/content/article/2005/09/15/AR2005091500915.html (accessed December 10, 2008).

[29]Howard Culbertson, "10/40 Window: Do you need to be stirred to action?" (June 10, 2008). http://home.snu.edu/~hculbert/1040.htm (accessed November 23, 2008).

[30]Elisabeth Freeman, "A Winning Idea: Ignite Your Faith," *Christianity Today* 67, no. 1 (January/February 2008): 11.

[31]Cam Beck, "The Meaning of Semper Fidelis," http://www.oo-rah.com/Store/editorial/edi52.asp (accessed December 19, 2008).

[32]Maggie Gallagher, "Corporate Resource Council: Why Supporting Marriage Makes Business Sense," *Family Life* (2002), http://www.familylife.com/atf/cf/%7B8E975F2E-4C1C-4315-AAFF-34A97EB367B5%7D/WP_Supporting_Marriage.pdf (accessed December 20, 2008).

[33]Jim Garamone, *Rite of Passage*, http://www.defenselink.mil/specials/basic/ (accessed December 21, 2008).